EFFECTIVE CHILD REARING

Child Development & Child Rearing Series

Childrearing Psychology
F. Wesley, Ph.D.

Childhood Learning, Behavior and the Family
L. C. Taichert, M.D.

Clinical Child Psychology
G. J. Williams, Ph.D. and S. Gordon, Ph.D.

Mother-Infant Interaction
C. E. Walters, Ph.D.

Parenting Skills (Manual and Workbook)
R. R. Abidin, Ed.D.

Learning to Play: Playing to Learn.
E. Bower, Ed.D.

Effective Child Rearing. The Behaviorally Aware Parent
F. W. Gosciewski, Ph.D.

The Abusing Family
R. Justice, Ph.D. and B. Justice, Ph.D.

EFFECTIVE CHILD REARING:

The Behaviorally Aware Parent

F. William Gosciewski, Ph.D.

Edinboro State College
Edinboro, Pennsylvania

HUMAN SCIENCES PRESS
Formerly **BEHAVIORAL PUBLICATIONS INC.**
72 FIFTH AVENUE, NEW YORK, N.Y. 10011 • (212) 243-6000

Library of Congress Catalog Number 76-3620

ISBN: 0-87705-262-X

Copyright © 1976 by Human Sciences Press
72 Fifth Avenue, New York, New York 10011

Printed in the United States of America
6789 987654321
Library of Congress Cataloging in Publication Data

Library of Congress Cataloging in Publication Data

Gosciewski, F William.
    Effective child rearing.

    Bibliography: p.
    Includes index.
    1. Children—Management.   2. Behavior modification.
3. Parent and child.   I. Title.
HQ772.G653   649'.1   76-3620
ISBN 0-87705-262-X

THIS BOOK IS DEDICATED

TO

SOPHIA ROSE GOSCIEWSKI

CONTENTS

5

FOREWORD

The area of behavior modification has expanded rapidly in the past decade and has now become one of the most important topics in the fields of mental health and education. Parents and teachers are now, more than ever before, being provided with information on how to effectively influence their children's behaviors toward the goals of self-realization, community awareness, and good citizenship. Parents and teachers of exceptional children are becoming increasingly effective in enabling these youngsters to overcome the sometimes awesome obstacles of exceptionality by means of highly structured and systematic remedial programs. The tasks of helping children realize their full potential, whether it be in the home or the school or the broader community, require an understanding of the nature of human behavior and a capability for utilizing that understanding to accomplish those goals. Behavior modification provides an important part of that understanding and facilitates the development of those capabilities.

In *Effective Child Rearing* Dr. Gosciewski provides the reader with not only a broad overview of those behavior modification principles and techniques most useful in parent-child interactions but also a clear understanding of the need for parent self-management as a basis for effective parenting.

While *Effective Child Rearing* is written primarily for parents, its utility extends well beyond that population. Educators will find it to be a concise and understandable introduction to behavior modification for classroom use; professional mental health workers will find it to be a valuable tool in teaching behavior management strategies to parents; students of psychology and education will appreciate its breadth and practical orientation.

In this compact book, Dr. Gosciewski has managed to integrate both the theoretical and applied aspects of behavior modification and to do it in a straightforward and concise fashion. *Effective Child Rearing* is a welcome addition to the educational and mental health literature.

JOSEPH J. COMI, ED.D.
Professor and Chairman, Department of Special Education, Edinboro State College; President, Pennsylvania Federation Council for Exceptional Children; Editor, P.F.C.E.C. Journal

INTRODUCTION

⌐ As parents we all have a common goal: that our children will gradually learn to be healthy and productive adults. We know that living successfully in society requires flexibility and strength, and that such attributes are the product of our ~~life-long~~ interactions with those who help us to meet our needs and to understand the needs of others. As we accept parenthood, we accept the responsibility for teaching our children to adapt to, and benefit from, the full range of human experience. The demands of parenthood are awesome, and the role of the parent must be looked upon from an intelligent and humanistic perspective.⌐

This book conveys the basic principles of an established system of behavior management (sometimes called behavior modification)—many of the techniques of which we all use to varying degrees. There is nothing new in the approach described in the following pages, but the organization of the well known principles of human behavior should enable you to improve your effectiveness role as a parent. This has been the reaction of many parents who have learned the behavioral approach to child management. A common observation of many of those parents has been that they have developed confidence in knowing what they are doing. They have developed a clear-cut point of view about behavior and they know, more than ever before, where they are going.

To the child development specialist, such reactions from parents indicate that positively oriented consistency in child management has begun. We all recognize that we are fearful about the unpredictable, and it is the fear of the unknown which is at the root of much of the undesirable behavior of all persons, especially children. Infants are not born knowing how to behave. They must be taught, or socialized, by their parents and by those significant others to whom they are exposed in the course of their development. It is consistency in these relationships that teaches the child that certain behaviors yield certain results, and enables him to predict and to regulate his behaviors accordingly. The behavioral approach fosters the development of a solid structure, within which your child can know what is expected and you can clearly communicate your expectations.

The basic idea underlying the behavioral approach is that all behavior is outcome directed. That is, you behave in the ways that you do because that's how you get what you want or need. If you decide to try something that you've never tried before, whether you will do it again depends on what you get for it. If you're alone the first time you light a cigarette, so that all you get is smoke in your eyes, a choking cough, and an upset stomach, the likelihood of your smoking again is decreased. If, on the other hand, you are with a group of smoking friends and your lighting up also results in greater attention and acceptance by the group, the likelihood of recurrence is increased. This basic principle applies across all human behaviors, and the older a person gets the more experiences he has had and the greater the complexity of his behavior. With the young, relatively inexperienced child, it is easier to see and to influence his developing behavior patterns according to that principle. The infant whose cries are followed by comforting parental attention learns to cry for attention. Discerning what any individual gets for particular behaviors is the starting point for influencing his behavior in desirable directions. Correspondingly, to the extent that you have control over what your child wants, to that same extent you have the capability of influencing his behavior.

At first, these principles of control may seem cold and clinical. However, if you look closely at your reactions to anyone's behavior, you will recognize that you do, often unwittingly, exert influence. Take, for example, the greetings that you exchange with a friend when you meet him on the street. If the friend greets you and you don't respond and that happens several times, it is likely that he will stop greeting you in the future. Your return of greetings maintains his greeting behavior. It is possible to analyze almost any behavior in terms of the give and take involved. The behavior management system enables you to organize your influence in such a way as to bring about desirable behavioral results in your children. That's what it's all about.

The behavioral management system is, then, a plan for productive interpersonal relationships. It is organized and precise, and the language of the system reflects that precision. You will find in the following pages that the language is not prosaic, and indeed is characterized somewhat by technical jargon. That will probably take some getting used to. You will notice that common words like "behavior" and "outcome" refer to specific events rather than to larger patterns of actions, as in everyday discourse. It is crucial that you understand the need for precision within the system in order to implement its procedures properly.

"Behavior," in this context, refers to a specific action that an individual performs or "emits". It is an observable, palpable phenomenon. You won't need to resort to less specific terms to convey your meaning. For example, if your older son is hitting your younger son, it is unnecessary and, perhaps, even harmful to describe the situation in terms of "aggression". Aggression is a conclusion we draw from observing behavior. It may be an accurate conclusion in a given case; or it may not. The point is that it is an unnecessary conclusion. If hitting behavior is hitting behavior, why do we need to call it something else? The significance of this distinction becomes clear when we decide to change that behavior. We don't work on aggression; we work on hitting behavior. If you do try to work with a concept as broad as aggression, precision flies out the window, and the consistency of the approach is lost. Without consistency, the system is destroyed and you're right back to the starting point.

A similar situation exists with the idea of "outcomes." Outcomes are specific events that follow specific behaviors, and that influence those behaviors in predictable directions. Outcomes are desirable, resulting in recurrence of related behaviors; undesirable, resulting in decrease in related behaviors; or not forthcoming ("zero"), resulting in corresponding decreases in behavior. Thinking in these terms, you may hug, spank, or ignore your child after he has kicked your dog. If your attention is significant to your child, you will see the effects of your behavior.

As you read through this book, you will find that I return repeatedly, both directly and indirectly, to the notions of consistency, predictability, and observability. These are critical considerations, particularly in working with children. Increased experience as we grow older enables us to understand the circumstances of our lives better, and to predict the results of our behaviors. In the young child, the ability to predict accurately in a variety of circumstances is less developed. It is a basic need of all children to improve their predictive powers. Such improvement in prediction will only result from consistent relationships with those persons on whom they depend. Teaching your children what behaviors will and will not meet their needs requires that you provide them with consistent outcomes following their desirable and undesirable behaviors. Correspondingly, you can only assess the effectiveness of your efforts by looking at those behaviors. Behavior—that is, *observable* behavior—is your only yardstick for measuring effectiveness.

It is also important to understand, as suggested above, that your behavior is influenced by its outcomes. And children can and do provide powerful outcomes. What you do following your youngster's behavior is influenced by what he does after that. In this regard, the important difference between you and your children is that you are better able to forego immediate needs as you work toward more distant goals. As a behaviorally aware parent, you can better understand your children's behavior and you can clearly define your objectives instead of proceeding aimlessly, wondering where you went wrong and what you could have done better.

I only mean to introduce these ideas here. They will be taken up and enlarged upon in the book where they relate to the methods being discussed. The behavior management system works. I have taught many parents and teachers the system in the last several years, and they have found that it works. What is more to the point, I suppose, is that it will work for your children, and for the adults they will one day be.

Chapter 1

PRINCIPLES AND STRATEGIES

People do what they do because of what they get for what they do. A child who touches a hot oven gets burned. Since he gets something he does not like, he probably will not touch the hot oven again. If instead he touches a table in order to brush off some crumbs, he may well receive praise and attention for being "Mommy's little helper." If he likes the attention from his mother, it is likely that he will try to be her little helper in the future.

This example represents a simple application of an idea that becomes increasingly difficult to apply as it becomes increasingly difficult to know the desirable outcomes, or rewards, that the individual seeks. Although it may not always be apparent, especially to the untrained observer, the disturbed person who behaves in unusual ways is always gaining something he thinks is desirable through his actions. The problem for the professional is to determine what's being gained.

As a parent, you have a similar, but not quite so complex, problem; that is, the key to understanding and effectively dealing with the behavior of your child lies in discovering and effectively managing his good and bad *outcomes.* If you can discover these, you can use them to control his behavior effectively, especially during his pre-adolescent years. As the child gets older, you will lose control of many of the effective outcomes because other persons in the child's life become increasingly important to the rewards he seeks to achieve. Adolescents usually spend less and less time at home and become increasingly dependent upon their friends and acquaintances for furnishing their broadening range of desired outcomes.

Over the years of growth and development continuing through adulthood, the individual learns, more or less effectively how to meet his needs. To the extent that his methods are effective and still socially acceptable, he is considered to be well-adjusted and, perhaps, successful. If he attempts to gain his desired outcomes through socially unacceptable means, his behavioral patterns are considered antisocial or maladjusted.

Depending on how things work out, the individual settles on patterns of behavior that are the most appropriate for him. The institutionalized mental patient who sits staring into space year after year-or exhibiting whatever other seemingly bizarre behavior—is also meeting his needs in the best way he knows how. Other sorts of efforts have met with repeated failure, and those around him, in attempting to meet their own needs, have not responded in ways that could have supported more desirable behavior patterns. In less extreme forms, virtually everyone occasionally exhibits depression, temper outbursts, isolation, dependency, "neurotic" behavior, and so forth. These behaviors, too, are outcome-directed. The person temporarily resorts to less appropriate behavior because of the likelihood that it will better meet his immediate needs.

Depression provides a good case in point. It may offer an effective way of justifying not doing something that the person believes he should do. The person's first need may be to behave responsibly, that need having been built in by previous experience. The need to behave responsibly, however, may entail time and effort which the person sees as undesirable. The second need, then, is to avoid the undesirable expenditure of time and effort. Since both needs cannot be met, a conflict arises, creating a third need: to resolve the conflict. This third need, which is the most immediate and pressing, is met by either (1) behaving responsibly or (2) behaving irresponsibly and using depression as the justification. Of course there may be other factors contributing to depression, such as physical status, but there is also the behavioral element: depression works in meeting a need.

The first lesson that a parent must take from an understanding that behavior is outcome-directed is that one's own sought-after outcomes must be discovered and understood. There is no reason to suppose that your behavior toward your children is not similarly governed. The mother who repeatedly screeches at her children may continue to screech because her other attempts to control the children's behavior have not worked, and screeching works, at least temporarily. The difficulty here lies not with the behavior of the children, however inappropriate it may be, but with that of the mother, who is meeting a need of her own in the best way she knows. It is unfortunate that in efforts to help parents deal more effectively with their children, the parents' needs are so often all but ignored. In fact all effective child-rearing methods begin with those needs.

In this book, you are encouraged to look at all your

behavior as a parent in terms of the outcomes you want or need. The following sections contain descriptions of the basic principles of behavior management that can help you to develop a good attitude as a parent and, along with it, an effective child-management approach.

The Reward Outcome

The basic element in the effective management of anyone's behavior is found in the consistently appropriate application of desired outcomes, or rewards. A reward is defined as any outcome which is seen *by the recipient* as desirable and which results in the reoccurrence of the particular behavior to which the reward is attached.

Primary Rewards

The more obvious rewards, such as food and drink, are desirable in that they meet the basic biological needs. Everyone demonstrates behaviors which have as their outcomes the availability and consumption of food. The more hungry an individual is and the less accessible food becomes, the more likely it is that he will behave in less typical and/or less socially acceptable ways in order to get the food. Conversely, the more satisfied the individual, the less likely it is that he can be influenced to behave so as to gain the food outcome. In getting the essentially satisfied individual to do something, therefore, another reward area must be used.

With younger children, an alternative food outcome area is available—sweets. If your children are in that age group, it is a good bet that they will behave in line with your expectations when you offer candy or soda pop as the reward. (I am reminded, however, of an elementary school teacher who used Life Savers as rewards for cor-

rect completions of arithmetic problems. She was puz-
zled when this strategy improved the work of all but one
child in the class. However, she soon discovered why the
boy failed to respond to such an apparently desirable
reward: his father was a Life Savers salesman!)

Object Rewards

Beyond the basic, or primary, rewards, there are several classes of desirable outcome which are effective in
supporting or reinforcing appropriate behaviors. One important area is that of tangible, or object, rewards: toys,
trinkets, hobby items, money, and the like. Obviously,
your child's behavior can be influenced when you give
him a toy, a game, or the like, to reward his compliance
with your wishes.

Activity Rewards

Another reward area involves desirable activities,
such as play. Permitting the child to go out to play only
after he finishes his homework is an example of the use
of an activity reward. The less desired activity (homework) tends to become more desirable by its association
with the more desired one (play).

Of course, you must handle this reward wisely to
make it work, especially in the beginning. If, for example,
you require too much work for too little play, your child
may reject the play so that he can avoid the work. If he
is then allowed to play later without first working, he
may well learn that play is achievable without working,
simply by waiting. At any rate, if you use reasonable
requirements, one activity can be quite effective in supporting the performance of another, which your child
finds less desirable.

Activity rewards are effective for children of all ages.

However, they are especially useful with older children, who tend to be involved in a wider range of activities both at and away from home.

Social Rewards

As a child moves through his early years, nearly all of his primary, object, and activity outcomes are provided by his parents. Since the parent often provides some social interaction or verbal behavior along with those rewards, the child comes to associate such parental gestures and verbalizations with the rewards themselves. After many such occurrences, those social elements come to take on the power of the other rewards. In effect, then, the social rewards become effective in supporting and influencing the child's behavior.

As time passes, the child becomes increasingly responsive to social approval and he no longer requires that material rewards follow every appropriate action. If the child's experience did not include such social interactions when other rewards were given, he would not learn to respond appropriately to the approval of parents and, later, to other significant people in his life.

Social rewards, then, are reactions from others which serve to strengthen the behaviors that they follow. Bearing in mind the apparent importance of these associations, you should pair all rewards with social approval. This will lead to the eventual increase in your use of social rewards and a corresponding decrease in that of other rewards. Your child will continue to receive social rewards from you and, increasingly, from others into adulthood and throughout his life. In fact, most typical adult behaviors can be demonstrated to have strong ties with the attention and approval of others.

Everyone looks to others for reactions to his behavior. In effect, people become what other people tell them they are through the other's approving and disapproving reactions. The child whose parents constantly criticize and belittle tends to develop feelings of inadequacy and unworthiness. Since the early development of socially appropriate behaviors is not met with approval and support, such a child may begin to resort to inappropriate behavior as a means of gaining at least some recognition of his capabilities. That child is behaving in the best way he knows in order to gain what he urgently needs.

Intrinsic Rewards

Many parents question the desirability of giving their children something to get them to comply with their wishes. "Why should my child be *bribed* to do things that I want him to do?" they ask. "Why shouldn't I just expect and demand that he do what is right?" These questions represent a frequent objection to the behavioral management system, and a clarification of terms is in order.

The term "bribery" is inappropriate in this context. Bribery involves giving something to someone for doing something which is not fair or is morally objectionable. Paying the traffic clerk to destroy a speeding ticket is a good example of bribery. Certainly, getting a child to complete his homework assignment by subsequently allowing him to go outside to play is not a similar arrangement. Parents do not bribe their children to get them to behave appropriately. What they do do is make appropriate activity worthwhile to the child until he, too, comes to see the behavior as appropriate, at which time he will no longer need constant parental support and encouragement in the form of these concrete rewards. This principle applies in all areas of parental influence.

Unfortunately, many children are placed by their parents in a position of avoiding punishment by complying with demands rather than working toward positive outcomes. There are many problems involved in this situation, the most serious of which is that the child will develop a negative attitude toward the demanded activity and will avoid doing it as much as possible. If he is threatened with punishment for not reading for example, the likelihood arises that he will never read any more than he has to in the future.

This discussion relates to what is ultimately the most important area of reward. The terminal outcome toward which all parenting should be directed is that of developing independent and responsible behavior in the child. The growing child who increasingly fulfills this parental objective is said to be coming to operate more and more in terms of intrinsic, or internalized, reward systems. That is, the individual behaves the way he does because he views the behavior itself as appropriate *and therefore* desirable.

This capability is similar to that of responding to social rewards. The child whose parents consistently reward him and approve of specific behaviors comes, by association, to value the activity in itself. Again, the activity itself takes on the strongly rewarding properties of other rewards with which it has been associated. The parent who reads frequently, enjoys it, and approves strongly of reading by his children, tends to develop similar reading preferences in them.

THE PUNISHMENT OUTCOME

While reward outcomes are meant to increase or maintain certain behaviors, punishment outcomes are designed to do just the opposite. When the young child runs carelessly into the street, his mother yells at him and may spank him. The *purpose* of her reaction is not to punish the child—or it should not be. The purpose is to decrease sharply the likelihood that he will behave similarly in the future and thereby endanger his life. The punishment, it must be kept clearly in mind, is a means and should never be made into an end. Punishment is the application of an undesirable outcome following the occurrence of an inappropriate behavior in order to end or decrease such behavior.

Like rewards, punishments can be administered in primary, object, activity, social, and intrinsic areas. For misbehaving, you can deprive your child of dessert, take away his toys, restrict his activities or reprimand him.

Punishment, especially when severe, can create problems, and therefore you should use it sparingly. As with rewards, associations take place when punishments are applied. If you subject your child to repeated and/or severe punishment outcomes following a given behavior, he will learn not only that that behavior is something to be avoided but also that the punishment situation and the person applying the punishment are undesirable and to be avoided. The child who does poorly in school and who is frequently punished and intimidated for his failings comes to view school negatively and to resort to behaviors designed to gain for him the desirable outcome of getting away from school. Dropouts and truants are examples of advanced cases of school avoidance problems stemming, at least in part, from a long history of punishment outcomes.

Punishment works quickly (though temporarily and inefficiently) and so people in a position to punish tend to rely too heavily on it because of the immediate reward *they* receive for using it. A parent seeking the desirable outcome of stopping his child's screaming may find spanking an effective behavior. If the child's screaming stops, the parent is immediately rewarded for spanking, increasing the likelihood that he will spank again in the future. Fortunately, most parents are socially and intrinsically rewarded for not physically abusing their children and that condition, along with the possibility that they too may be punished, tends to check excessive use of physical punishment. Non-physical forms of punishment, however, are not always so well controlled.

It is quite likely that inappropriate and disproportionate use of punishment is the single most important cause of behavior problems in children. Punishments for certain behaviors without alternative reward outcomes for other behaviors fails to teach the child how he should behave in order to meet his needs. The likelihood is therefore increased that the child will make more behavioral mistakes, leading to more punishment, avoidance, inappropriate behaviors, and so on.

It is, of course, very unlikely that you could totally avoid the use of punishment in parenting. If used appropriately and with moderation, punishment can be an effective outcome for influencing appropriate behaviors in children. A discussion of the appropriate use of punishment is provided below and in subsequent chapters.

THE ZERO OUTCOME

The zero outcome requires that the parent do *nothing* following any particular behavior that a child may exhibit; the purpose being to decrease or get rid of that behavior. The child whose cries get him parental attention learns that crying is an effective means of getting that attention. Under normal circumstances this is appropriate and necessary, especially for the child who cannot yet talk. However, if the child stubbornly cries when put to bed, attention supports this behavior and it can become a problem. Once sure that there is no danger or physical discomfort to which the crying can be attributed, one way to get the child to sleep without problematic crying is to remove the child's sought-after outcome—attention

—which has been forthcoming in the past. The child's first reaction will be to cry still more, but if the parent is consistent in not providing the outcome, the child will eventually learn that crying no longer works and he will stop that useless behavior. The zero outcome, then, calls for the elimination of a typical outcome response by the parent. The difficulty of course is that the stopping-of-crying outcome is desirable for you, and in the past you will have been rewarded by that outcome for going to the child. What is required, then, is that you forego the immediate reward for a long-range one—and that, often enough, in the face of considerable pressure.

An even more trying situation is seen when a child resorts to crying and temper outbursts in public as a means of gaining a desired outcome. In this situation you are subject to social pressure to stop the unruly behavior. An easy way to gain the immediate cessation of crying is to give in to the child, but the problem is then sure to come up in future public situations. Again you may have to sacrifice some immediate outcomes in order to gain the more enduring desirable outcome.

Putting Outcomes Together

In the public situation described above, most parents who do not give in to the child will apply one of two possible outcomes: they will ignore the child's outbursts (provide a zero outcome) or they will punish the unruly behavior (providing an undesirable outcome). Either parental reaction, particularly the former, may gain the beleaguered parent his immediately desired end, but neither is sufficient for the most effective management of the situation—nor are both together. In any situation where the child exhibits inappropriate behaviors, it is best and strongest to utilize a combination of outcomes, working toward supporting appropriate kinds of behavior as well as decreasing or eliminating the inappropriate behaviors. Let us say that you want your child to be well behaved, and perhaps helpful, in a shopping experience. This is best accomplished by ignoring or punishing the misbehavior *and* rewarding appropriate behaviors in that situation. If you know for example, that the child wants candy or some special item, you may elect to give him the item after he has behaved appropriately for a given period of time. This will teach the child that simply asking and behaving appropriately is the way for him to get what he wants; whereas demanding and crying will lead to nothing or to undesirable outcomes. Many parents fail to follow through with rewards for good behavior after providing zero outcomes or punishments for bad behavior, thus teaching the child what he should not do but not what he should do.

Many parents who have busy schedules themselves will tend to pay a lot of attention to the child when he demands it in the form of some inappropriate behavior. They then wonder why the child misbehaves so often, never realizing that they have taught him the most effective ways of gaining their attention. If the parent concentrates on regularly attending to the child and providing his known desirable outcomes when he is behaving appropriately, then the child would not have to become unruly in order to get his needs met. This combination approach is the cornerstone to the effective management of children's behavior.

Special Considerations

You will have recognized, of course, that there is really nothing new in what has so far been presented. We all use rewards, punishments, and zero outcomes in dealing with everyone in our experience. If we are at all insightful, we also use outcome combinations with varying degrees of effectiveness. The real value of the behavioral management approach is not in its novelty, but rather in its *systematic* application of the principles of behavior change.

A basic need of all persons, but especially of children, is to be able to predict with some confidence what the results of their actions will be. Through experience the child learns to anticipate outcomes of his actions, enabling him to choose behaviors which will most likely lead to the outcomes he desires. If those who deal with children do not behave in a consistent manner, the child will remain confused about how he should behave. The result is all too often that the child will endlessly try to determine what the outcomes will be—he "tests the limits." Contained in this testing-of-the-limits are many of the behavior problems about which parents express concern.

In applying combinations of outcomes there are certain considerations that should be kept in mind.

Prevention

It really goes without saying that preventing problem behavior is preferable to correcting it. This will be seen as especially important when you know that problem behaviors tend to encourage other problem behaviors, as good behaviors tend to create more of the same. If you can anticipate problems, you will have more time and energy to work on building good behaviors rather than stemming the tide of troublesome ones. In Chapter 5 "the behavioral attitude" is discussed as a means of anticipating difficulties and catching behaviors before they get out of hand. Any parent who gains a good understanding of the principles of effective behavior management should be in a far better position to be prevention-oriented.

A simple example of the preventive approach is seen in the case of the young husband whose wife was about to have their first child. This young man knew that infants tend to cry as a means of communicating their needs to their parents. He decided that it would be worth the effort to try to anticipate the needs of his child-to-be and to attend to them before crying became necessary. He decided that he would attempt to go to the child in the morning as soon as he heard the child moving about, which was an indication that the child was awake and would soon be crying for attention. He and his wife followed through on this plan consistently and as a result the infant seldom cried after awakening in the morning. The young father had taught the child that simply moving about would bring the attention wanted; crying would not be necessary.

To go beyond this, it can be suggested that good behavioral management of a youngster while he is small is of utmost importance for preventing many of the potential problem behaviors as the child progresses through the stages of development. Many parents of teenagers who have had repeated difficulties with their children are overwhelmed by the prospect of establishing influence with a child who has never been properly trained to respond favorably to parental expectations. In fact, it's never too late, but getting a good start contributes incalculably to making a good finish, and it makes everything in between far less difficult.

Behavior

When you are involved in managing the behavior of your children, your concern is with what the child actually does; what the behavior is, and not what it represents. Many parents refer to their children as "immature" or "aggressive" or "disobedient" or by any of a number of other vague terms. When applying the behavior management system, it is crucial that the focus be on specific actions. If you are concerned that your older son is repeatedly striking your younger son, it is not necessary, and it may be confusing, to discuss and deal with that behavior in terms of "aggression". It is more nearly precise, and far more useful, to look at hitting behavior as hitting behavior. When the time comes for influencing the child not to hit his younger brother, then it is easy to determine whether the child is exhibiting the behavior which is being worked on. If instead you attempt to work on his "aggressive behavior", it will be far more difficult to know when and how to apply the appropriate consequences consistently, and consistency is critical to success. Any attempt to deal with a child's behavior should be made only after you know specifically, in behavioral terms, what that behavior is. Anything else will only create confusion and leave the child uncertain as to what he is and is not expected to do.

In addition to making the specific behavior more easy to deal with, you may be surprised to find after you have carefully defined the behavior that it is not so bad as you had thought. The author is reminded of the first-grade teacher who described a child in her classroom as "very immature" because she was "always crying". After she was encouraged to be very specific about the behavior and to watch for that specific behavior, she discovered that the child in question never cried more than twice in any three-day period. Several other children were found to cry more frequently and yet she had never thought to describe them with the same term. It became apparent that other specific behaviors contributed to the teacher's "very immature" impression. The groundwork was thereby laid for that teacher to work more effectively with other specific behaviors that were in need of modification. If she had been advised to provide reward outcomes for "mature" behaviors and to ignore or punish "immature" behaviors, it is unlikely that any real progress would have been made due to the lack of behavioral clarity.

Modeling

Children imitate their parents, as any observant parent can certainly confirm. It is apparent that an excellent way to develop appropriate behavior in children is to demonstrate effective behavior in parenting. In fact, since the effective parent tends to be the effective person and vice versa, it can be said more generally that the person who controls his own behavior is capable of effectively influencing the behavior of others—and especially that of his children.

The child whose father reacts to frustration and difficulty by having temper flare-ups can be expected to exhibit similar behavior in frustrating and difficult situations. If the child is then punished for such outbursts, he becomes confused about the double standard—which can lead to quite deep confusion about imitating other parent behaviors, no matter how appropriate they may appear.

Beginning

Children's behavior is built step-by-step. The child who is exhibiting several problem behaviors today cannot be expected to behave totally differently tomorrow. Your beginning efforts should be small and within the reach of the child. Behavior must be gradually reshaped to new patterns through consistent, patient modification of pieces of the total pattern.

The child who grumbles about school (for example) and fails to perform up to reasonable expectations may, in the beginning, have to be provided with favorable outcomes when he simply studies. Once that first step has been successful, he may be rewarded for improvement—*gradual* improvement—of specific results in separate subject areas. To offer rewards to a poor student who gets nothing beyond D's and F's only for the attainment of A's and B's is bound to fail, and to create additional problems for both child and parent.

Success and reward are the most effective building blocks for continued success at higher levels. It is your job to prepare the way towards maximum success at increasingly difficult levels, and this is best accomplished by starting with big rewards for small performances and gradually increasing the performance standards while decreasing the reward allowances. Underlying the possibility of doing this is the need for dealing with specific behavior parts which contribute to the total pattern.

Outcome Selection

We have said that reward outcomes are those that the child sees as desirable, and that result in reoccurrence of the specific behaviors to which they are attached. Parents often make faulty assumptions about what a child considers to be desirable because of interference from their own preferences, and also their ideas as to what is "good for" the child. To the extent that rewards of any sort are not in line with what the child wants, they will fail to support the modifications in behavior that the parent wants. Some parents are accurately described as treating their children as "miniature adults," and one of the ways that is done is in expecting children to appreciate things that adults consider appropriate and desirable. But of course children are not miniature adults.

In selecting reward outcomes, then, you must take

care to provide things which are seen by the child as desirable and worth changing for. This can be accomplished either by asking the child or by observing what rewards the child selects on his own. As an example, if the child frequently watches television, it can be assumed that he enjoys it; that is, that he considers television-watching to be desirable; and this activity may be used as one of the rewards for target behaviors. Care should be taken, though, to provide a variety of possible rewards so that the child does not tire quickly of any one.

Punishment outcomes may be selected in the same way, by observing what the child resists doing or getting and taking away or restricting what you already know the child sees as desirable. Particular care should be taken in selecting the intensity and duration of punishments. Some parents restrict children for a month, or remove television privileges for two weeks, following the occurrence of some inappropriate behavior. Such long-term punishments tend not to work as well as more intense, short-term punishments because the child, after a few days, loses the connection between what he did and what he is being required to do. What results is that the child develops bad feelings toward the parent and growing resistance to parental controls. In such a situation it might be better to restrict the child for a day or two *and* to disallow all TV privileges during that time. The younger the child is, the less likely he is to benefit from long-term punishments. With age comes increased verbal ability, and with that increased capability of understanding relationships for longer periods of time.

Timing

As is suggested in the preceding section, timing of rewards and punishments is critical to their effective use. The closer in time that the act and the outcome are, the more effective the outcomes tend to be. If a mother tells a child, after he has committed some negative behavior, that his father will punish him when he gets home from work that evening, the child is more likely to learn to fear his father than to connect the inappropriate act with the long-delayed punishment. Particularly in supporting new or improved behaviors in the child, you should be certain to provide immediate rewards. If the particular reward, such as an activity, is very difficult to administer at that time, a substitute or "token" for that reward may be provided with the understanding that the token will later "buy" the desirable outcome in question. The token economy, discussed in Chapter 3, provides a means by which such substitute reward systems can be established.

Reward Shifts

Social rewards should always be administered along with primary, object, and activity outcomes. The purpose of this is to get the child to associate the power of other rewards with social approval, thereby making social approval more rewarding in itself as the child grows older. Obviously, the teenager cannot be rewarded with a piece of candy or a toy when he washes the car or cleans the basement; but he may be given the opportunity to use the car or have his friends over for a get-together in the basement.

More importantly than that, though, the teenager should be led to perform specific behaviors or tasks at least in part simply because his parents approve of his actions. The older the child becomes, the more responsive he should be to such approval. The keyword there is *led*— without having prepared him for that stage, you will accomplish nothing by abruptly saying to him "No more object rewards, now you start doing it just because I'd approve of your doing it." This shifting of rewards is accomplished by pairing social with other reward outcomes and *gradually* removing the other outcomes while keeping the social rewards in effect. It is a good idea to continue to use primary, object, and activity outcomes, but less and less frequently.

The shift from other outcomes to intrinsic rewards will take place in the child if the other reward outcomes are managed effectively by parents. Everyone demonstrates at least some intrinsic reward systems, depending upon the nature of his reward experiences through childhood.

Follow-Through

Once you've decided what behavior you want changed and the specific outcomes to be used, it is very important that you follow through with the plan. Children will usually resist change in their experience because at first it decreases their ability to predict the outcomes of their behaviors. It is then your responsibility to establish a new consistency and to maintain it even though the child may not immediately respond as you'd like.

When parents are asked what they have tried in order to make changes in their children's behavior, many respond, "Everything." They have probably failed to follow through with one or two well thought out plans of behavior management. The result is often confusion and increased behavior difficulties in the child and frustration and increased punitiveness in the parent.

The lack of quick and favorable response is especially common in situations where the zero outcome is applied. Suppose that your child has, in the past, cried repeatedly until you finally responded with attention. If you decide one day to stop responding to such cries, it is very likely that the child will cry more vigorously than ever. Real resolution will be required. If you follow through with your zero-outcome plan (including giving the child attention when he is not crying), you can expect the crying to get much worse—and then to stop rather abruptly. It is in the period where the child makes his last, all-stops-out effort that most parents give in. This failure to follow through is a serious error which will make the eventual correction of the inappropriate behavior still more difficult to achieve.

One young mother's two-year-old boy screamed and cried and clung to her leg whenever she talked on the telephone. After five to ten minutes of this behavior, the mother would get off the phone and scold the youngster for interfering with her conversation. In fact, the boy had gotten what he wanted—his mother's undivided attention. If she had ignored the boy's attention-seeking behavior, it is quite likely that he would have persisted for several more minutes. If she followed through beyond that time, and on *every* telephoning occasion the child would eventually learn that such behavior would not get him what he wanted. Failing to follow through even *once* after the zero-outcome plan had been started might result in quite amazing persistence by the child. Again consistency is crucial: correcting this problem situation requires that the mother get off the telephone *only* when the child is not exhibiting the problem behaviors.

Cues

To get your children to behave in accord with your expectations, it is obviously necessary that you let them know what those expectations are. Too often, children are reprimanded even though they had never been made aware of what was expected of them. The responsibility for that behavior must be placed with the parent.

As the child comes to know in general what's expected of him, there is less need to tell him specifically —to cue him for appropriate behaviors.

A cue is a signal to the child that a specific action is called for *and will result in a desirable outcome.* Calling the child for supper or telling him that it is seven o'clock (time for homework) are simple examples. A common error in this facet of behavior management is failure to follow through with the outcomes which the cues signal. For example, the mother of a ten-year-old boy called him to dinner. The mother came out the front door and, seeing her son several feet away talking to a friend, called to him in a pleasant voice. When the child did not respond, she called in a somewhat less pleasant fashion. Again, the child gave no response. The mother then called more loudly and with some threat in her tone. The boy turned toward her for a moment and then went on talking to his friend. Finally, angered by his lack of compliance, the mother took several steps toward the boy and called him in a very loud and severe tone. At this point, the boy turned and responded to his mother's request. This situation represents a misuse of cues. In the past the boy had apparently taken advantage of his mother's failure to follow through in enforcing compliance after only one or two cues. It required a display of anger on the mother's part for her to gain her desired outcome. That is, the boy had learned that no undesirable outcome was likely to follow until a certain degree of anger was evident.

Many psychologists and child management specialists suggest that parents talk too much to their children and do too little. The child is quick to learn that undesirable outcomes (leaving one's friend in the example) can be postponed by ignoring impotent cues. If you want your cues to be effective, you must act on them promptly— and, to ensure that they remain effective, consistently.

Communication

The suggestion that parents talk too much and do too little may want clarification. It is not meant to recommend that you not talk to your children; but only that you have some care not to talk too much, or too little, or at the wrong time, such as in the cueing example given above. Communication is an on-going process. Parents let their children know that they are accepted and approved of as individuals who can behave appropriately and improve themselves in a mutually beneficial relationship. The parents communicate the structure, the expectations, and the outcomes involved in living together. In turn, they listen to their children and respect their individuality as they guide them through the often confusing and frightening process of growing up.

In this communication process the parent must remain in authority, demonstrating confidence in his own ability to provide the child with structure and guidelines for desirable and undesirable behavioral tendencies. The child then can look with confidence to the parent for direction in his behavior. A salient feature of the behavioral management system is that it fosters confidence in the parent as he gains consistency and direction in carrying out his parental functions.

Finally, it is important that you not seek out bad behaviors to be changed. If a problem presents itself, then it is dealt with. If not, your orientation should be positive —toward helping your child as he continues to move in the direction of growth and development. Positive expectations for children tend to foster positive behaviors in them.

Chapter 2

APPLICATIONS

Chapter 1 was meant to introduce the basic components of the behavioral management or modification system. A general understanding of those principles is necessary for comprehension of their applications, as presented in this chapter. What follows is a presentation of such applications across a wide range of behaviors commonly encountered by parents. Application examples are presented first, of establishing, increasing, and maintaining desirable behaviors in children, and second, decreasing and eliminating undesirable behaviors.

PROMOTING DESIRABLE BEHAVIORS

The situations described in this section are selected from among the most typical areas of concern expressed by parents to the author over the past several years of psychological consultation.

Situation 1   Self-care toilet habits

The first consideration in any toilet-training program is with whether the child is yet physically ready
to control the functions related to bladder and bowel
elimination. It has been suggested that infants go through
being aware that they have wet to being aware that they
are wetting to being aware that they are going to wet. Not
until the last stage, usually reached somewhere around
two years of age, is the child ready for toilet training
procedures. If the procedures are instituted too early,
there is likely to be excessive and demoralizing failure,
leading to emotional reactions becoming associated with
the elimination process.

Once you are reasonably sure that the child has
reached the required stage of physical awareness, you
may begin to orient the child to bathroom functions. This
should be done in gradual stages and without pressure for
quick success.

The following arrangement plan does not present all
of the details involved in carrying out the toilet training
procedure, but it should serve as a guide for an effective
program.

STEP 1.   Provide models. The child should be given op-
portunities to observe his parents and/or siblings en-
gaged in elimination. Children like to be like their older
brothers and sisters and their parents in as many ways as
possible. The opportunity to see a desirable model performing a new function should establish the desirability
of the action in the child's mind and provide incentive for
him to do likewise. This modeling procedure can, of course,
begin long before the more formal aspects of training.

STEP 2.   Place a potty chair in the bathroom near to the
commode. The child will explore the new object and

probably will voluntarily, at one time or another, sit on the chair. If not done spontaneously after a good length of time, you might mildly suggest such an experiment. In either case, when the child does sit down, the outcome should be a display of great approval and even joy. The child will discover that simply sitting down leads to a very desirable outcome.

STEP 3.   When the child is being bathed and remains in the bathroom unclothed, watch for and, if necessary, encourage the sitting behavior again. Follow such behavior with liberal praise and, perhaps, a highly desirable primary reward.

STEP 4.   By now, you should have spent some time observing what the child's elimination patterns are. Having learned them, take the child to the potty shortly before an expected elimination and enthusiastically ask him if he wants to try out the potty like mommy or daddy. If he resists, do not apply pressure and try again at another time. If he complies, praise and reward liberally.

STEP 5.   After several instances of potty elimination, gradually eliminate the primary rewards and continue with social rewards. Gradual movement to the toilet should be encouraged and rewarded. Patience and gradually raised expectations should prove effective. Most importantly, keep the situation relaxed and positive, especially in the early stages.

Situation 2   Going to bed on schedule

Children of all ages characteristically resist going to bed if they are not adequately prepared to accept the inevitable. Allowing the child to be playful and become excited just before bedtime and then presenting an abrupt demand that he go to bed is almost certain to breed resistance or, at least, muted expressions of anger and resentment. No one wants to leave a situation when it is at its peak of enjoyment. Another consideration is that parental directions which are not enforced create in the child an expectation that he can resist further. When a bedtime is agreed upon, except under unusual circumstances it should be adhered to for the welfare of all concerned.

STEP 1.   Determine an acceptable bedtime for the individual child, taking into consideration his particular rest requirements. Too early and too late times are likely to create problems for both child and parent for obvious reasons. Modifications of the schedule are appropriate as the child gets older (though flexibility on individual nights should not be very much increased until adolescence—once a new time is established, it should be adhered to). Such changes can be effectively introduced as rewarding outcomes.

STEP 2.   Gradually lower the activity level several minutes prior to the scheduled bedtime.

STEP 3.   Cue the child in advance. Five to ten minutes prior to taking or sending the child to prepare for bed, let him know that he has just a few minutes left. The aim is to avoid surprising the child and thus triggering spontaneous resistance.

STEP 4.   Announce to the child that bedtime has arrived and follow through immediately. Do not permit the child to delay and dawdle unreasonably because these may well be small beginning steps toward bigger resistance attempts.

STEP 5.   Spend some time with the child, particularly the younger child, once he is in bed, to end the day on a positive note. Praise and several indications of approval of the child's cooperative behaviors are appropriate at this time. This time should not be used for discussing problems with the child or reprimanding him for past misadventures.

Situation 3   Cooperative play in the young child

Conflicts and occasional aggressive outbursts are common among young children. Such occurrences are not only inevitable, they are necessary to the child's developing social awareness and adaptability. Your aim should not, therefore, be to eliminate these altercations totally. On the other hand, the child can benefit socially by gradually more cooperative play experiences with siblings and friends. You can be supportive in this regard by encouraging positive directions in play. General guidelines for supportive intervention are provided below.

STEP 1.   In playing with the child yourself, you can demonstrate cooperative sharing and respond favorably to him when he shows any tendency to share and cooperate. You must understand, though, that the young child is basically self-oriented and will naturally demonstrate behavior that in an adult would be thought unacceptably selfish.

STEP 2.   You should intervene as little as possible when distruptions occur between or among playing children, allowing them to resolve their differences and learn from the struggle to resolve them. The hovering parent is likely to reward dependent behaviors in children and thus to curtail movement toward cooperative play patterns.

STEP 3.   Playing children can discreetly be observed and you can enter the situation with praise and special rewards when they are getting along well. Intervention at times of conflict, on the other hand, encourages more conflict.

STEP 4.   Approving discussions of the child's good play behaviors can be conducted later in the day, particularly at meal times. Obvious parental approval without accompanying criticism leads the child to seek additional approval through his behaviors in similar situations.

STEP 5.   Particularly for the only child or for the child who is much younger than his siblings, ample opportunity should be provided for the child to interact with his age-mates. Age-appropriate behaviors are best learned by experimenting and comparing with peers.

Situation 4   Appropriate table manners and eating habits

Just about every parent expresses concern, at one time or another, about his child's eating habits and/or general table conduct. In most families meal times, and particularly the evening meal, are among the most significant times of total family interaction. These times should be kept as pleasant and free from conflict and criticism as possible since they contain great potential for forming positive—or negative—associations between primary food outcomes and general family interactions. Regular unpleasantness at these times can not only disrupt eating patterns, but can also create serious difficulties in basic communications and family relationships.

STEP 1.   Provide appropriate models. As in so many other situations, the child can be expected to imitate his most significant models. The model that says one thing and does another can expect to get inappropriate and, sometimes, unexpected responses.

STEP 2.   Provide reward outcomes liberally as the child eats a variety of foods and makes early efforts to handle his utensils in increasingly effective ways.

STEP 3.   Provide zero outcomes when the child rejects foods for no apparent reason and when he manipulates his foods in less effective ways than you have previously seen him demonstrate. Avoid as much as possible punishment outcomes for troublesome behaviors. Occasional suggestions and encouragements when the child is having difficulty are appropriate.

STEP 4.   If an older child behaves unreasonably, he could be directed to leave the table with the following comment. "Go into the other room. When you think that you can act like the rest of us, you may return." No other comments or lectures should be given. When the child returns, he should be accepted without comment. As he behaves more appropriately, he should be given approving comments or signs.

STEP 5.   Be flexible in your requirements. Like anyone else's, children's appetites and tastes vary and children should not be forced to conform to your personal likes and dislikes. Make the food attractive and provide variety.

STEP 6.   Follow through. If it appears that the child is being unreasonable in any given situation, do not force the issue; handle it calmly and systematically. Then when mealtime is over, do not permit snacking soon afterward. You must teach the child that he cannot do as his mood dictates and get desirable outcomes regardless. It is usually a good idea to prohibit all snacking for two hours or so after the meal has ended when there has been a problem. Depending on the severity of the situation, it may be necessary that snacking be disallowed for the

entire evening. However, this should only be done infrequently and in especially difficult situations; the line between zero outcome and punishment outcome is a thin
one. It should not be crossed, especially in connection
with food, except in acutely troublesome situations.

Situation 5   Good study habits

Developing good study habits in children takes time
and depends upon the child's seeing studying as desirable
and necessary for gaining other desirable outcomes.
Above all else, the child should not come to view homework with dread. To the extent that he does, similar to all
other situations which are considered to be highly unpleasant, he will attempt to accomplish only the minimum in the shortest amount of time required—to "get it
over with." This preoccupation will seriously damage
concentration and lead to habitually low output.

Encouraging the child to develop more desirable attitudes and habits related to studying is done by providing
highly desirable outcomes for small beginnings and gradually requiring more production for less obvious rewards. The ultimate objective is to enable the child to
become intrinsically rewarded for this otherwise unpleasant task.

STEP 1.   Since so much of homework requires reading,
the parent who himself reads and enjoys it will tend to
have children who do, too. Long before the necessity for
homework, when the child is very young, the desirable
nature of reading activities should be established.

STEP 2.   Homework requirements should begin small
and be strongly supported by the parents as enjoyable
activity. Parent and sibling participation in the young
child's homework is appropriate so long as such involvement is positive and oriented to success for the child's

beginning efforts. Too often the adult in this situation becomes frustrated at the child's slow progress and he destroys the enjoyability of the process by expressing that frustration to the child. The situation becomes aversive; the child will later avoid it whenever he can. In general, if you cannot tolerate the slow pace without disapproval you should not participate in it, or terminate participation when you reach your limit. The author has seen all too many homework situations end in tears for the child and, sometimes, the parent.

STEP 3.   As you become aware of the kinds of skills your child is working on and what concepts he is learning, you may be able to use those same concepts in your other interactions with the child. For example, if he is learning subtraction, you might send him to the store and allow him to figure out the appropriate change, and give him liberal praise and approval if he does. (Good judgment is required here. The aim is to make the application of his new skill rewarding; it is not to associate still another new responsibility with homework, nor is it necessarily to get the right answer at the store.)

STEP 4.   Structuring time into the daily schedule for homework and other required behaviors is usually effective in avoiding conflicting desires in the child. When he knows that 6 to 7 P.M. is consistently set aside for homework, he will not schedule competing activities and create unnecessary conflicts. It is usually advisable for other members of the family to use the same time to do things which will not interfere with the child's responsibility or make him feel that he is missing something desirable by performing what will then become more unpleasant. During that time, father and mother might watch the news, read the paper, or do something else neutral to the child.

STEP 5.   As the child gets older and homework requirements become more stringent, you should continue to take an interest in what he is doing. Homework is not an isolated activity. It relates to all areas of academic performance, and that relatedness should be kept in mind as a positive aspect of the child's educational growth. Too often the requirement for homework by both parents and teachers comes to be associated with punishment. The teacher who assigns additional homework for low performance or misbehavior, or who assigns less homework as a reward for better performance, is misusing homework and fostering the child's perception of it as undesirable.

Situation 6   Personal neatness and hygiene

Children who leave clothing lying around the house and who fail to maintain personal appearance to a reasonable degree of neatness usually do so because their parents reward them for doing so. The parent who picks up after the child teaches him that his own picking up is not necessary; it may even be rewarding if the parent focuses a good deal of attention on that fact. Criticism for not doing something is generally much less effective than praise and rewards for doing it, especially if the criticising parent ends up doing it himself.

STEP 1.   Reasonable expectations must be established: responsibilities must be within the child's capabilities. Then he must be informed of precisely what you expect. This may involve encouraging the child to do something and following that with praise or other desirable outcomes. Particularly with the younger child, frequent reminding or cueing may be required. Care should be taken when this is done to avoid lecturing or repeating the direction unnecessarily. A simple and firmly pleasant reminder should suffice.

STEP 2.   If the child periodically forgets, as he certainly will, you might remind him and allow a reasonable time for compliance. Personal rigidity, where the parent demands immediate compliance, should be avoided because it leads to power struggles and ensuing bad feelings in all concerned.

STEP 3.   When the child fails to follow through with picking up or grooming, do not confront him with the failure and force him to do it. Rather, application of either a zero outcome or a mildly undesirable outcome is called for. You may, for example, just leave the item where it is without comment, or you may take the item and keep it from him beyond the time when the child needs it. The "Sunday–Box Technique", discussed in Chapter 4, is one way of handling such failures effectively.

In the case of grooming, hand-washing may be required before dinner. Favorable attention should be given when the child follows through. When he fails to do so, he is at first reminded and, later, not permitted at the table until he complies satisfactorily. Again it is crucial that these strategies be executed with minimal talk, pleasant firmness, absolute consistency, and ample reward for cooperative behavior.

STEP 4.   Under no circumstances should you take over the responsibility for the child. This becomes increasingly important as the child grows older and becomes more capable of managing his own affairs.

Situation 7   Being on time

Unlike adults whose livelihood and personal effectiveness may depend significantly on time-consciousness, the child is often oblivious to the hour and the day.

Socializing a child means, in part, making him increasingly aware of and responsive to the expectations and needs of others. Specific time schedules usually do not become a concern until the child is of school age. However, once the child is on his own to a certain extent, he must become sensitive to such regulations and respond in a reasonable fashion. Similar to all of the other situations presented, if the child does not experience appropriate undesirable consequences for lateness and, more importantly, appropriate desirable outcomes for promptness, he will fail to learn the appropriate behaviors.

STEP 1.   The parent of the preschool child should not allow himself to drift into the pattern of having to call his child repeatedly in order to get him to respond. This could well be the beginning of time-related problems later on. In these early stages, the child should be called once or twice or, at most, three times. As indicated in Situation 2, it may be advisable to let the child know ahead of time that he will be called shortly as a means of getting him ready to respond. If you allow yourself to be ineffective by not actually requiring the child to respond reasonably when he is called, you are teaching him that compliance is really only required after delay and, perhaps, parental expressions of anger. If this situation does develop and the parent is angry by the time the child comes, it is likely that the child will be received angrily. This is an undesirable situation (outcome) which may well result in even longer delays as the child tries to avoid that outcome for as long as he can. This would be an example of an inappropriate use of an undesirable outcome.

STEP 2.   As implied above, the child's coming when called should be met with mildly desirable outcomes in order that that behavior is rewarded and maintained.

STEP 3.   As the child gets older and extends his activities beyond the home setting, he should be given reasonable time limits and expected to obey them. Occasional difficulties are to be expected and the parent should be reasonably flexible in that regard. However, if there is an apparent lack of compliance, then the parent should firmly and from the beginning show mild disapproval without undue lecturing or scolding. Again, the rewarding of compliance should accomplish most of the objective.

STEP 4.   If the situation appears to be worsening because of prior inconsistent management, then the parent may have to make an arrangement with the child whereby he will receive obvious advantage from being prompt and obvious disadvantage from being late. The token economy system discussed in Chapter 3 and the contract system discussed under "Special Techniques" (Chapter 4) would apply in making the situation more workable.

STEP 5.   Eventually the child should honor time commitments because, it may be assumed, he has developed empathic regard for the people around him. In other words, he has come to operate through intrinsic motivation. Social and other rewards should then be used occasionally as a means of keeping the intrinsic reward effect strong.

Eliminating Undesirable Behaviors

Similar to those presented thus far, the situations described in this section are selected from among the most typical areas of concern expressed by parents.

Situation 8   Temper tantrums and crying

As we have seen, behavior has a purpose, it is out-come-oriented. This is never more clearly seen than in tantrum and similar crying behaviors. Typically the outburst is designed to gain for the child an outcome which he considers to be otherwise unattainable. Through that behavior or behavioral pattern, the child creates stress for the parent so that the parent is forced to seek a desirable outcome for himself—that is, the cessation of turbulence or crying. Too often under these circumstances the nonbehavioral parent may respond inconsistently, sometimes giving in and other times becoming punitive, thereby unknowingly giving the child sought-after attention. Such unreasonable behavior may begin when the highly frustrated child tries out this technique as a last resort in order to gain some desirable objective. If the parent gives in at that time or in other early attempts, he is ensuring that the child will return to that effective behavior in the future. The more effective that behavior is, the more the child will rely upon it.

STEP 1.   Since the parent is the primary model for the child who is learning how to deal with his environment, he must take great care not to demonstrate tantrum-like behavior himself in order to gain his own outcomes. If this is characteristic, more or less, of either parent, it must be changed before effective changes can be expected in the child. Parent self-control is necessary in this as in all other aspects of management.

STEP 2.   If the tantrum behavior has been exhibited over a long period of time, the parent may be able to anticipate such situations and avoid them by giving the child what he wants before he resorts to the tantrum, thereby showing him that tantrums are not always necessary, or by refusing the child's demands at a time when tantrums are least likely to occur. Immediately prior to the child's going somewhere or doing something desirable might be an appropriate time.

The problem with this approach is that many tantrum behaviors are more or less spontaneous and it is not always possible to avoid the difficult situation. In addition, this is not really so much a solution to the problem as it is an avoidance of it. For those reasons, the following steps would usually be preferable.

STEP 3.   When the tantrum is beginning or in progress, it is imperative that you not provide the child with his desired outcome. If the outcome will eventually be applied and the child is reacting to the time he must wait, you must be sure that he gets what he wants only after some desirable, non-tantrum behavior. This should be far enough away from the tantrum that the child does not make a connection between his tantrum and the desirable outcome.

The alternatives available are, first, to provide a zero outcome (ignore) and, second, to provide an undesirable outcome (punish). The first alternative is usually preferable because if you punish you may unknowingly be giving the child what he wants—attention, even though it is negative attention. Once you decide to ignore the tantrum, you must never, except under the most extreme circumstances, change your approach. If you do so after five tantrums, you are teaching the child that the next time he wants something it will take five tantrums to get it.

An important factor about which it is fair to warn you is that in using zero outcomes, at first the behavior will probably get worse. This is to be expected because the behavior has worked for the child in the past and he has become convinced of its effectiveness. When this happens, many parents tend to give up, saying, "Here I am doing something to improve the behavior and it only gets worse!" It is crucial during the worsening phase that you continue the plan. The apparent worsening of the behavior will disappear—perhaps even quickly, but not necessarily—as the child discovers that his efforts are no longer successful. As a result, your confidence will—at last!—begin to grow that the approach is effective and that the behavior is on its way out.

If and when you cannot allow the tantrum to continue for reasons of safety or property damage, the only alternative then is to punish decisively and with as little emotion as possible. Immediately after the punishment is administered, the ignoring is begun again. In this way, the chance for inadvertant rewards is minimized. This procedure must be followed, without exception, for as long as it takes to eliminate the undesirable behavior.

STEP 4.   Using the combination approach discussed in Chapter I, the parent must be sure to provide the child with desirable outcomes when he attempts to gain his outcomes through more appropriate means. When the child is obviously frustrated and does not resort to tantrums or crying, the parent should comment on that fact approvingly and provide some alternative desirable outcome. The child must be taught not only that will he not get what he wants through inappropriate behaviors but that appropriate behaviors will gain desirable outcomes.

STEP 5.   The most difficult aspect of this approach is for you to control yourself in the face of what is clearly a very unpleasant situation. Parents, too, operate according to the principles of behavior and it is natural for them to want to stop the undesirable situation as quickly and effectively as possible. Unfortunately, the best way is not always the quickest and you must learn to postpone your own desirable outcomes just as you expect your child to postpone his. With this consideration in mind, you must not give in and you must remain as obviously unemotional as possible. To do otherwise is to worsen the problem and extend its duration.

STEP 6.   With the older child who is sometimes more difficult to ignore and/or punish, you must determine what outcomes desired by the child you have control over. Management of the situation is then constructed around more or less availability to the child of those outcomes as the child behaves more or less appropriately. A point system (Chapter 3) or a contractual arrangement (Chapter 4) may be structured wherein the child expects and knows what he is gaining through his actions. Once such a system is instituted, it must be followed consistently and firmly. If you can remain relatively unemotional, avoid talking too much, and follow through on the planned outcomes, then you can expect the child finally to terminate his unproductive behaviors.

Situation 9   Thumbsucking

Thumbsucking is a common and natural occurrence among many children which does not really become a problem until parents unknowingly reward it. Positive experiences tend to become associated with other things which are happening and are present at the same time. That is, being fed becomes associated with oral stimulation and with mother. It is not too surprising that the child would want to extend those happenings (oral stimulation through thumbsucking) and stay in the presence of those objects (mother) because of the associated reward (food). If left alone, thumbsucking will discontinue by itself because it will no longer be associated with feeding and no longer needed for comfort as the child learns new ways to meet his needs. Unfortunately, many parents see thumbsucking as a sign of "insecurity," whatever that is, and fear the disapproval of others who may draw the same inappropriate conclusion. As a result, they attempt to convince the child, in one way or another, to stop that behavior and thereby provide him with a desirable outcome—their attention—for continuing it.

STEP 1.   Ignore it. If it was not ignored from the outset and has become a chronic behavior, then ignoring it and reacting positively to decreases in thumbsucking as time goes on will add strength to the alternative action.

STEP 2.   As a variation of Step 1, you may, in addition to generally ignoring it, occasionally display mild disapproval of that behavior. This should be done without comment by, for example, a facial expression. Again, this variation carries with it the potential for unintended rewards through attention.

STEP 3.   As the child gets older and increases his social contacts, there will be other sources of disapproval for the "immature" behavior which is more likely to be effective than parental disapproval in that the child wants to be like and accepted by his peer group.

STEP 4.   In the event that the child's thumb becomes blistered or otherwise irritated or there are other physical repercussions, you may be forced to use some form of punishment or restriction. In that event, the combination approach with very mild punishment would be most appropriate. Again, great care must be taken to punish with minimum chance of the child's being gratified by the attention.

Situation 10   Bedwetting

This is a very difficult problem to deal with and most approaches suggested by mental health professionals thus far have been less than impressive. The primary reason for that is the difficulty in determining what a particular child's desirable outcomes may be. Some suggest physical causes, some behavioral causes, and most recognize a probable combination of factors. Ultimately it is up to the parent himself to make the final determination of the reasons for continued bedwetting. In this regard, and from the behavioral viewpoint, the parent is strongly advised to avoid attributing significance to "insecurity" or "anxiety" or the like. Bedwetting is a behavior and should be treated as the problem and not as an indicator of a problem about which nothing can be done.

STEP 1.   Proper toilet-training procedures provide the best prevention. Whether the condition develops in spite of apparently adequate training procedures or because of inadequate ones, the first consideration is with the potential for physical difficulties. Therefore, the parent who is concerned with this problem should first get medical assistance to rule out a physical predisposition. If such results are negative or inconclusive, then the following process is generally appropriate.

STEP 2.   Reasonable precautions can be taken with respect to what may be increasing the possibility of such incidents. Restricting liquid intake prior to bedtime is most appropriate, and this should be accomplished without undue discussion with the child as to the reason for it. Again, such attention and obvious concern may be desirable and rewarding to the child. In addition, precautions against physical damaging results can be taken. Removal of the bedspread and use of a waterproof mattress cover should be accomplished unostentatiously and without any emotional overtones.

STEP 3.   On occasions of bedwetting, the child should be made as responsible for clean-up as his abilities allow. Stripping, washing, and re-making the bed are all advisable. If the child fails to comply with such requirements, then the bed should either be left in its soiled condition or the items removed and left in an obvious place for the child to consider. This is done without comment or emotionalism.

STEP 4.   Special efforts should not be made to assist the child in changing his behavior. Using special gadgets to awaken the child who is wetting or resorting to waking the child periodically throughout the night will probably be counterproductive in that responsibility for controlled elimination is taken away from the child. The added danger of inadvertant rewards is also apparent.

STEP 5.   The only time any attention is directed to the general situation is when the child successfully and progressively sleeps without incident. In that case, praise and other desirable outcomes should be applied and made clearly the result of the successful sleep period.

STEP 6.   If the situation has been a very difficult one for a very long time, you may utilize the token economy system with appropriate rewards combined with zero and/or mildly undesirable outcomes. This approach is fraught with complications and is not advisable unless the problem has not been resolved by the previous steps applied over a long period of time. The constant attention contains reward potential, for one thing, and then there is the knotty problem of determining what outcomes are supporting the behavior. In such a situation, the fewer attention-directed strategies that you use, the less likely that the behavior will be unintentionally rewarded.

Situation 11   Speech difficulties

Children learn to speak by listening to those around them. Unless there is a physical problem, the child will become as effective in such communication as the availability of desirable outcomes will support. The parent who uses inappropriate speech and fulfills his child's needs in response to inappropriate speech teaches the child to speak inappropriately. The author is reminded of several instances of children who entered kindergarten or first grade with obvious speech irregularities and, to their parents' surprise, quickly changed their speech patterns when they discovered that they could no longer meet their needs effectively until they changed their speech.

STEP 1.   Providing appropriate speech models is essential. Continuation of "baby talk" beyond the early stages of infancy is likely to create confusion in the child because of inconsistencies in expression of those around him. The gradual development of language in a child is an amazingly complex accomplishment, and unnecessary variations only add to the immensity of the task.

STEP 2.   If, for other than physical reasons, the child develops faulty speech patterns, the parent should require gradually improved speech. Requests made by the child in faulty speech may be met by less ready response than when minor improvements are observed. "Wa" to "wawa" to "wata" to "water" represents a simplified example of a gradual improvement in the child's requests which would be met by gradually changing responses. Care must be taken to be reasonably certain that the next level of demand is within the child's capability. Too rigid requirements for the very young child can be demoralizing. For any child, consistent modeling and strong approval reactions for better speech productions are appropriate.

STEP 3. In addition to what is suggested above, you should not direct unnecessarily obvious attention, such as lecturing and scolding, to the inappropriate speech productions. A calm, matter-of-fact approach in conjunction with good outcome arrangements is likely to be most effective.

Situation 12   Lying

Accomplishment of immediate needs without adequate consideration of long-term outcomes is characteristic of the younger child. With this in mind, it is not surprising that a child who is confronted with a situation that may lead to an immediate undesirable outcome would resort to behaviors which would enable him to get out of the stressful situation as quickly as possible. Lying is such a behavior which may offer short-term gains and, less importantly to the child, long-term problems.

STEP 1. It's wise to avoid creating situations where lying may be seen by the child as a way out. The parent who knows that a child has done something unacceptable and asks him if he did it is putting the child in such a situation. If you already know what has occurred do not ask the child if he did it, but rather tell him that you do not approve of what he has done. If you're sure, denials by the child should be ignored and you should follow through with those outcomes you consider appropriate to the situation.

STEP 2. If you are not convinced that the child is responsible for some action, do not accuse the child or "interrogate" him in order to discover the truth. An indication that such an action is inappropriate regardless of who committed it would be a better alternative. That way the child knows what outcome will follow such unacceptable behavior if he is found to be responsible in future situations, and he is not pressured to lie about such possible involvement in that situation.

STEP 3.   If the child later informs you that he was in fact responsible, then you should not punish at that time. If punishment were to follow such a truthful admission, that admission and not the unacceptable act would in fact be the punished behavior. Therefore, you should praise the child for his truthfulness and indicate that the behavior was inappropriate and would in the future result in undesirable outcomes.

Many parents who suspect that a child has done something will badger the child until the child finally admits his guilt. The admission is then followed by punishment and, as a result, the child learns that it is better to persist in his denials in the future. Such continued denial typically involves additional lying and the child will then discover that lying does work, that is, it provides desirable outcomes through avoidance of undesirable outcomes. In addition, in the process of questioning and accusing the child, the situation is full of possible unintended attention rewards, possibly resulting in the increase of other inappropriate behavioral tendencies. This would include the communication to the child that the parent expects the child to lie and commit other undesirable behaviors. Such expectancies tend to support such behaviors.

STEP 4.   As the child learns that lying is neither necessary nor effective, you should constantly provide desirable outcomes for coming to you and being open about anything, including the desirable and undesirable things he may have done.

STEP 5.   If lying behavior has been a persistent problem over a long period of time, begin management as suggested above. Initially the child will continue to lie when forced to and you must begin to take care to avoid such situations and to provide desirable outcomes for any movements toward increased communication by the child. Unnecessary and unproductive discussions about the problem should be discontinued. All expressions of anger, disappointment, and threat should be eliminated. Changes may take a long time, but your new consistency of appropriately arranged outcomes will work.

Situation 13   Attention-getting

Children often demand control over parental attention in various ways. The toddler may constantly interrupt or cry or otherwise force you to stop what you may be doing and direct your attention once again to him. The circumstances are very similar to those described in Situation 8.

The author had occasion to work with one young mother whose child would constantly hang on her leg crying and whining. When she attempted to talk to a neighbor or to use the telephone, the youngster would raise such a fuss that continued communication was very difficult. Typically this mother stopped what she was doing and focussed her attention on the child, either positively or negatively. In effect, the child was very successful in his efforts and he persisted at an amazing rate.

STEP 1.   It must be demonstrated to the child that the behaviors in question will no longer work. You must ignore or calmly punish such incidents with a minimum of attention to the child.

STEP 2.   Timing is crucial. When the child has stopped, even temporarily, his attention-getting behavior—and only then—you should attend to him.

STEP 3.   As in other strategies, the critical element for successful elimination of the inappropriate behavior is to provide desirable outcomes for competing behaviors. In this situation, the competing behavior is non-tantrum behavior, and the parent must attend to the child when he is behaving reasonably well. The parent must go to the child when he is quiet and cooperative and demonstrate that that behavior leads to desirable outcomes.

Situation 14   Sibling rivalry

As indicated in Situation 3, all children will, and really need to, have disagreements with other children as a part of learning how to relate more effectively as they mature. Sometimes, however, such altercations become extreme to the point where they disrupt the entire family and set the stage for other conflicts and disturbed relationships. In such cases, it is necessary for the parent to intervene and bring the level of conflict into more reasonable bounds.

Since some guidelines for this situation are provided in Situation 3, a more specific conflict is dealt with below so as to illustrate an effective strategy. The situation involves two children who repeatedly fight over objects and privileges and two parents who typically handle the disputes by intervening, deciding whom the object belongs to or whose turn it is, and imposing their decision as a resolution.

STEP 1.   In the situation presented where the children continue their disputes despite parental efforts, it appears likely that each child has learned with experience that loud disputes will bring the parent (and his attention) and that the parent may well provide him with the disputed object or privilege at the other's loss. Since no parent is likely consistently to decide in favor of one child or the other, both have been rewarded on an intermittent or irregular basis for such conflict behaviors. Researchers have learned that irregular rewards tend to create more persistent behaviors in children than regularly predictable ones. That is why parents are encouraged to develop an occasional reward approach after the child has developed a desirable behavior by regular and consistent reward outcomes.

Considering this situation, therefore, it appears that the children's behavior is being maintained by two desirable outcomes: regular attention rewards and irregular object and privilege (activity) rewards. The combined effect is apparently desirable enough to each child to outweigh any undesirable elements in the parental involvement, such as scolding.

The first thing the parent must do under these conditions is to eliminate intervention as much as possible so that the children can learn to resolve the disagreements themselves.

STEP 2.   When the disputes become destructive and intolerable and necessitate parental contact, such contact should be made quickly and without too much talking and emotional reaction or attention.

STEP 3.   The cool, quick contact is designed to demonstrate that no one will benefit when the parent intervenes. Therefore, rather than making a judgment as to who does and does not win in the situation, the parent makes sure that both lose by removing the object in question from both children. If the object is a certain toy or game, the parent simply removes it and places it into an inaccessible area. If the dispute is over television programs, the television is turned off.

Once the removal of the object or activity is accomplished, the parent leaves the situation immediately and goes back to non-involvement.

STEP 4.   As the children are observed playing cooperatively together, the parent should enter the situation and provide approval for such appropriate efforts by both. At that point, the parent may return the item to the children and, again, allow them to determine how it will be shared. In effect, the parent both rewards cooperative play and permits independent problem solution.

STEP 5.   In the event that such conflicts continue after the parent has been consistent over a reasonable period of time (perhaps several weeks), then the children may be receiving other undetermined desirable outcomes for the behavior. In that case, the parent will have to resort to additional desirable and undesirable outcomes arranged in contract or token economy form so as to reduce the influence of the undetermined outcomes. The children must be taught that such disputes are not effective in gaining desirable outcomes, which are available through more appropriate behaviors; or, they may be shown that such undetermined desirable outcomes are not worth the increased undesirable outcomes which follow the disputes.

Situation 15   Adolescent defiance

As the child grows older and becomes increasingly capable of meeting his own needs, the influence of parents becomes less significant, unless the parent has been effective in establishing appropriate intrinsic reward systems in the child. To the extent that the parent has been unsuccessful in getting the child to behave appropriately because he wants to and, correspondingly, to the extent that the parent has relied on punitive controls, he can expect his child to resist such controls as he becomes more self-sufficient.

The parent of the adolescent who refuses to comply with parental wishes and demands is in a very limited and stressful situation. If he wishes to establish or maintain control, he must assess what controls he has left and make the best possible use of them to teach the child that appropriate behavior is worthwhile and that defiance and non-compliance will be costly.

STEP 1.   Assuming that the situation is already out of hand, the first decision you must make is what objectives you want to accomplish with the youngster. There are usually several behaviors which are troublesome, and it is best to define them carefully and to determine reasonable and achievable limits for such actions. For example, it may be that the child is repeatedly late, staying out well beyond what the parent considers to be a reasonable time. In this event, the parent will have to assess just what a reasonable time is and establish limits within that framework. A similar determination can be made for other problem areas.

STEP 2.   After the parent knows what reasonable demands he wants complied with, he is ready to see what he can use to teach the child that compliance is worthwhile or rewarding and that non-compliance will be undesirable or costly. Such things as the availability of car insurance, access to the car, allowance, new clothing, clothing maintenance, typical home privileges (TV, telephone, etc.), food, parental approval, and anything else over which the parent retains control should be considered. Many parents assume that they have to fulfill their basic responsibilities to the child even though the child fails to be responsible to his parents. In fact, the more severe the adolescent defiance, the more willing the parent must be to utilize the basic elements of influence. In this regard, however, you must remember that your proper goal is to establish reasonable influence with the child for his welfare with your own welfare taken into account. Such influence must not be used to create a subservient child, but rather to foster responsible behavioral tendencies in a young adult.

STEP 3.   Once you know what you want and what you can use to get it, you are in a position to provide desirable outcomes for reasonable compliance and undesirable outcomes for non-compliance. This can best be accomplished at that age level through informal contract arrangements or through establishment of a token economy or its equivalent.

STEP 4.   As in other management approaches, the best orientation is a positive one. Excessive use of undesirable outcomes and corresponding emotionalism creates more problems than it solves. You should not threaten the child with the loss of something if he does (or fails to do) something. You should rather offer him something desirable when he does something desirable. In effect, the child has the option of acquiring something he wants (and may previously have gotten for nothing) simply by abiding by reasonable family regulations.

STEP 5.   To ensure reasonableness for all concerned in the family situation, it is best to discuss the responsibilities, expectations, and desires of all concerned and to reach some mutal agreement on what is fair. If this is done with the youngster and he recognizes the reasonable nature of the situation, he will tend to comply more readily and to expect and accept the various outcome arrangements.

Chapter 3

TOKEN ECONOMY

The token economy is a system of behavioral management which has demonstrated effectiveness in a wide variety of settings, including the home. Parents who have adopted the system have typically reported significant positive changes in the behaviors of their children—and of themselves. The systematic nature of the program enables the parent to establish, perhaps for the first time, a consistent management scheme, fostering confidence in themselves and a clear understanding of parental expectations in their children.

The economy is based on the principles of reward, punishment, and zero outcomes, in combination. In effect, the child is paid (rewarded) and fined (punished) for behaviors which the parent has determined to be desirable and undesirable, respectively. Under the system, the parent is directed to list specific behaviors to be increased and/or decreased and to make performance/nonperformance obviously valuable to the child. The limits of effectiveness of the system are determined by (1) whether the child can understand the basic ideas involved and (2) whether the parent is in a position to control outcomes meaningfully. The very young, non-verbal youngster and the older, physically large and effectively defiant adolescent are examples of individuals with whom the system may not be effective. In such instances, the individual strategies discussed in Chapters 1, 2, and 4 might be more appropriate.

STRUCTURE

In setting up the token economy in the home, you must be careful to design it with adequate consideration of the particular child and his unique behavior patterns. Failures of the system are usually caused by ill-considered selections of behaviors and outcomes. Provided below are guidelines for structuring the economy in line with good principles of behavior management.

Selecting Behaviors

The first step in setting up a token economy is to select the behaviors to be increased in frequency and those to be decreased or eliminated. In this phase you must be sure to specify the behaviors clearly and in terms of the observable actions involved. To talk about decreasing "aggressive behavior" or increasing "good manners" is vague and will likely create confusion in both you and your children, leading to failure of the system. On the other hand, specifying the behaviors as "hitting a younger brother or sister" or "brushing teeth three times per day" is an easily observable and clear-cut behavioral description, allowing parents and children alike to know exactly what behaviors are under consideration. With this important consideration kept in mind, select no more than four or five behaviors in each category, the desirable and the undesirable. The list may look something like this.

Desirable Behaviors
1. Doing homework 1 hour per evening
2. Brushing teeth 3 times per day
3. Being on time
4. Saying "please", "thank you", and "excuse me"
5. Practicing piano ½ hour

Undesirable Behaviors
1. Picking nose at dinner table
2. Interrupting adult conversations
3. Biting fingernails
4. Hitting younger brother/sister
5. Talking back to parents

Once the behaviors have been decided upon and you are satisfied that everyone concerned will understand specifically what behaviors are referred to, the next step is to select positive or desirable outcomes which the child will have the opportunity to earn.

Selecting Reward Outcomes

Reward outcomes (as always) must be selected with the child's, not the parent's, particular preferences in mind. They will only be effective in supporting good behaviors if the child considers them to be desirable and worth working toward. Two basic types of outcomes should be specified: (1) short-term rewards which the child can "purchase" immediately or almost immediately, and (2) long-term rewards which the child can work toward over a longer period of time. Short-term rewards may include such things as getting out of doing the dishes, visiting a friend's house for an hour, having a special snack or candy, being allowed to use a tape-recorder for a half hour, and so forth. Long-term rewards might include special activities which can only happen, for example, on weekends or once a month or whatever, and cannot therefore be administered at once or very soon, or they may be objects which are of greater cost which the child cannot be given very often. In either case, the long-term reward involves considerable value and/or time and is viewed by the child as so desirable that he is willing to work toward it for a longer period of time due to its greater cost or point value. Some examples of long-term rewards are: staying overnight at a friend's house, going to the Saturday matinee at the local theater, getting a bicycle, going to summer camp, going hunting or fishing with father, having a "free day," getting a new dress, and so forth.

In selecting reward outcomes, it is advisable to consult the child and/or to observe his stated and selected activities and objects. You should avoid offering only those outcomes which you consider to be "better" for the child, assuming that none of his chosen outcomes is actually harmful. The author had occasion to work with one parent who used money and allowance outcomes. The child revolted and rejected the system when the parent insisted on putting seventy-five percent of the reward into the bank for the child, against the child's wishes. When the child is given an outcome, it is imperative that he have control over its disposition. To do otherwise is not to give it to him at all, and defeats the purpose of the system.

Once several reward outcomes in both the short-term and long-term categories are agreed upon, it is time to assign positive and negative point values to the desirable and undesirable behaviors already selected and to specify the point cost necessary for each of the short-term and long-term reward outcomes.

Assigning Point Values

Especially in the early applications of the token economy, extreme care must be taken to ensure that the child can rather easily earn enough points to gain access to the reward outcomes, particularly the short-term ones. The child must be shown in the beginning that it is worthwhile to make small changes in his behavior. If the reward outcomes are too remote, calling for extensive effort, the child will tend to reject the new approach right off. You will gradually require more effort for the reward outcomes once the child is convinced that working for such outcomes is effective and worthwhile. The author is reminded of a situation with pre-school children in a day-care facility where the professional personnel rewarded the children for clean-up activities with pennies. To their dismay, the children did not respond at all well to the system. One day the teachers took the children to the dime store and allowed them to purchase whatever they wanted with the few pennies each child had accumulated. After the opportunity to experience the real value of their tokens (pennies) the children worked tirelessly to earn more rewards for future use. The now highly desirable pennies were easily accessible to the children for rather minor clean-up tasks, and they were considered to be well worth the limited effort by the children. The day-care instructors gradually required more effort for the same amount of pennies and eventually eliminated pennies for other tokens and, later, for just social approval and praise. It worked out very well.

So, working out specific point values and point costs should be done with these considerations in mind. First, the point values for desirable behaviors should be lower when the behavior is easier and can occur more frequently. For example, if the behavior under consideration is the child's saying "excuse me", "thank you", and "please" at appropriate times, then the point value should be minimum due to the simplicity of the behavior and due to the possibility of such behaviors occurring several times during any given day. Assigning a value of one point to this behavior establishes a base value to work from. For doing homework for one hour, on the other hand, the point value should be considerably higher due to the greater time and effort involved. One possible guideline is to assign one point for every five minutes or so that the behavior involves. In this case, then, the homework hour would be worth twelve to fifteen points. The desirable behavior list might, finally, look something like this when points are assigned.

Desirable Behaviors	Point Values
1. Doing homework 1 hour per evening	12–15
2. Brushing teeth 3 times per day	3 each
3. Being on time	10 (minus 1 for each min. late)
4. Saying "please", "thank you", "excuse me"	1 each
5. Practicing piano ½ hour	6–10

Using this example, it can be seen that the child who accepts the system and works in earnest might earn from fifty to seventy-five points, more or less, per day. In the early stages of the economy, however, the child may earn at a much lower rate. In whatever case, it must be kept in mind that early in the system the cost of rewards must be kept low so as to maximize the likelihood that the child will be rewarded for small beginnings.

The second area of consideration involves taking away points for bad behaviors—and the estimated loss of points must also be taken into consideration when determining the amount to be charged for reward outcomes. In this situation you must determine how each listed undesirable behavior will be valued for penalty purposes. In general, it is best to keep penalty values low, especially in the beginning. If the child loses too many points early in the system he will likely become discouraged and reject it. A guideline for applying values to the undesirable behaviors is similar to that for the desirable: the more frequently an undesirable behavior occurs, the less it should be valued. This applies if the high frequency undesirable behavior is not too serious; if it *is* serious and occurs often, then higher point costs should be applied so as to bring it down quickly. Punching a younger brother or sister, with the serious possibility of actual physical harm, might be one such instance. Typically, however, the stated guideline will apply pretty well.

With these considerations in mind, the undesirable behavior list might look like this.

Undesirable Behaviors	Point Values
1. Picking nose at dinner table	1
2. Interrupting adult conversations	2
3. Biting fingernails	1
4. Hitting younger brother/sister	5–10
5. Talking back to parents	5

In this example, it can be seen that early in the system the child could lose, perhaps, twenty to forty points or more per day. This is—and must be—less than what he will have the possibility of earning in one day.

Once the arbitrary point values for desirable and undesirable behaviors have been set, you are ready to select
and assign point costs to the short-term and long-term
reward outcomes. As pointed out above, you should take
care to select rewards that will be seen by the child as
highly desirable and to assign cost values that are easily
within the reach of the child. As the child becomes accus-
tomed to the system and sees the value of working toward
his desirable outcomes, the cost values can be increased
as a means of getting more desirable and less undesirable
behaviors at a lower cost rate and a higher social reward
rate.

In the example used above, it was estimated that the
child could earn with relative ease in one day approximately fifty points for desirable behaviors and that he
might lose about thirty points for undesirable behaviors.
Therefore, if the reward is to be "purchased" at the end
of a given day early in the program, the cost should not
exceed twenty points for any short-term reward. Correspondingly, for rewards that the child may select during
the day, when he has not as yet accumulated so many
points, the cost should be lower still, probably in the
five-to-ten-point range. Long-term rewards should probably not cost more than five days' possible points or, in this
case, about one hundred points; and in fact, considerably
lower cost should be considered so as to allow the child
access to both short- and long-term reward outcomes. The
more he can get early in the program, the more powerful
its impact will be. If the long-term reward is several
weeks away, say eight weeks, then the cost should certainly not exceed eight hundred points and, much more
favorably, would probably best be in the area of three to
four hundred points. Such a determination will have to
depend on the nature of the reward itself and the early
response of the child to the system. You should be flexible
and generous in such determinations, particularly in the
beginning.

Following the same example given above, the reward list and corresponding point-cost values could take this form.

Short-term Rewards	Point Cost
1. Special snack-of-the-day	5
2. Watch special TV program before bed	10
3. One hour later stay-up	15
4. Skip dishes	10
5. Skip routine chores	10
6. Listen to stereo - ½ hour	5
7. Telephone privilege - ½ hour	5

Long-term Rewards	Point Cost
1. Saturday afternoon movie	30
2. Overnight at friend's house	75
3. New bicycle	800

In looking over the rewards and respective point-cost values, you will see that the child cannot earn all of them in any one day, or in any one week. This is important in order to decrease the possibility that the child will tire of the rewards, robbing them of their desirable and motivational properties. It is a good idea to vary the rewards and to restrict repeated access to any single one. For example, snack purchases might be limited to two per day, thereby encouraging the child to select other ones and to keep the rewarding power at a high level.

In sum, assigning point values to specific reward outcomes, both short- and long-term, must be done after you consider what the child wants and how much his wanting it will result in desirable changes in his behaviors. The more difficult it is for the child to make change in his behaviors early in the program, the easier it should be for him to be successful in gaining desirable outcomes by making small changes. As change becomes easier, the increased demands for change are reflected in increased point-cost values. Extreme care must be taken to do this gradually, always making sure that the child is moving within the limits of his capability toward highly desirable goals. Other special considerations for effective application of the system are provided below.

APPLICATION

Once you've structured the system in line with the guidelines provided above, you are ready to introduce it to the child or children and to begin operation. In the early stages of application, you should remain flexible and willing to modify the system as you see its weak points and get better ideas for making it effective. Such changes will depend on the characteristics of the children and parents involved and on the specific resources available in the situation.

Introduction

The first step in application is to introduce the system to the child and to explain it to him in detail so that he knows what is expected and what outcomes are available. Ideally, the child should respond to the system willingly and with enthusiasm. To the extent that the child has a negative reaction to the plan, he will have to be shown the desirability of the system by making powerful rewards easily accessible. In either case, present the system firmly and with conviction. If the child totally rejects the system, he must not be provided with any of the desirable outcomes specified in the program. Chances are that as you remain firmly consistent the child will gradually yield. In any event, you must remain calm and firm and explicit in presenting the plan. It may be advisable to ask the child for additional ideas on how to improve the system, especially the outcomes, to make it more workable.

The token economy involves the use of several paper forms. (Models of these are presented later in this chapter.) As the system is introduced to the child, he should be shown the forms and their use should be explained.

Beginning

Once the child understands the system and any initial changes have been made, the stage is set to begin. Forms should be completed with the appropriate behaviors and outcomes and their respective point values. Forms should be posted on a bulletin board, refrigerator, wall, or some other public place in the home. You should have your own records straight and ready for entries.

Beginning on the next Monday after the system has been presented and all forms prepared, point counts should be kept for all desirable and undesirable behaviors and reward outcomes should be provided.

In the first few weeks of operation it is quite likely that there will be mistakes and, perhaps, controversies over points earned and lost, and so forth. It is always difficult to make a comprehensive change in family routines, and parents and children alike should not become too easily discouraged. With practice and special efforts early in the program, it will soon become routine itself. At that point, the system can be most effective and rewarding. Probably the best way to prevent many of the minor difficulties likely to be encountered early in application is to keep exact records. When points are granted or taken away, they should be recorded *immediately* and not left to memory for convenient moments. It is amazingly easy to forget situations and point dispositions, especially if more than one child is involved. Many parents with whom the author has worked have found it valuable to carry a record notebook with them at all times, facilitating good record-keeping. In any event, minor problems will undoubtedly occur and the best way to get past the early stages is to make special efforts at that time.

Transitions

As the system moves along, it will be necessary to make transitional changes as the child improves and seeks new outcomes. As a behavior is corrected or established, it should be dropped from the list and replaced by another one. The child should be advised of your approval regarding the improvement and told that he may get occasional "bonus" points as he continues the appropriate behaviors, even though that particular behavior is no longer in the system proper. This is a good way of phasing out certain behaviors and maintaining their improved status as new improvements are in the works. Similarly, new reward outcomes should be introduced so as to keep the system "fresh" and geared to the child's changing desires. You can improvise in several ways. For example, some parents and teachers have used "reward menus" from which the child is given an opportunity to select among a large variety of reward outcomes, including daily or weekly "specials". Children respond well to novelty and it's very helpful to invent variations to keep the system attractive and exciting.

Tokens

An alternative approach to just awarding points, especially with younger children, is to use an actual money form or tokens. Under this approach, the child is actually "paid" with tokens and the need to keep precise point records is minimized. Poker chips or special buttons or printed currency or other objects work well and tend to add to the rewarding effect. Just as adults like to see some of the money they earn, children like to receive something concrete for their efforts. You may want to try both approaches and decide on the one that seems to work out better. One parent with whom the author was acquainted used real money and reported that the effect was significantly better, but that the children tended to become very money conscious. The parent was concerned about the possible ramifications as the children got older. In general, special tokens would appear to be more advisable, but, again, that depends on the parents, the children, and the nature of the situation.

Variations

Other improvisations may be considered by the parent who wishes to keep the system interesting and, possibly, educational. For example, token bank accounts may be established and checking accounts may be designed. Even bonds and stock, with their related economic principles, could be utilized. Such investment procedures are particularly applicable with long-term reward situations. At the end of each week, for example, the excess tokens could be invested for long-term outcomes. If the parent suggests an "interest" factor, the child may well be learning to postpone his gratifications more effectively. Such postponement capability is an important aspect of growing up anyway, and parental support in this area can be very effective in getting the child to become less impulsive and more effectively oriented to desirable goals in the distance. Of course, all such variations call for time and effort on the part of the parents, and they are only advisable if they do not create needless stress which would work against better total family adjustment.

Termination

The token economy is not recommended as a permanent system in the family structure. The basic purpose is to develop in the child greater socialization through more effective behavior patterns based on responsiveness to social and intrinsic reward systems. Therefore, as you operate the system you should certainly apply social rewards along with the points or tokens and, later, concrete reward outcomes. The aim, finally, is to decrease use of the system and to depend more and more on the social reward procedures. The more effective the system is, the shorter will be its formal application.

The elimination of the program should be done gradually, with behaviors and rewards being removed from the formal structure over a reasonably long period. Just how long a reasonably long period is depends on the continued need for it and the reactions of the children to the discontinuation of dependence upon it. I can only advise you to see what works and adjust accordingly. Some parents have terminated the system for a few weeks and then returned to it several times. Each termination period was extended until the return to it eventually just never came.

Regardless of how the system is terminated, it is critical that the use of concrete reward outcomes not be eliminated entirely, but only decreased in importance relative to social rewards. Special care must be taken to avoid falling back into the patterns which supported the old undesirable behavior.

FORMS

In this section are provided models for three forms that have proven to be useful in the home token economy.

Make use of all or any of them, depending on the specific nature of the economy you elect to establish. Several other form models can be found in behavior management publications, many of which are listed at the end of this book.

Weekly Behavior Chart

The Weekly Behavior Chart is designed to organize specific desirable and undesirable behaviors to be dealt with and their corresponding point values. This chart is based on the weekly system approach, which has typically been found to be the best time unit with which to work. Of course, daily charts may be substituted, but this adds to the considerable bookkeeping already called for by the token economy program, and is usually unnecessary.

Looking over the Weekly Behavior Chart, you will see that in addition to spaces for the desirable and undesirable behaviors and corresponding points, there are spaces for keeping track of points spent, keeping a current balance, and keeping a record of long-term points accumulated over previous weeks. As previously noted, it is advisable to keep all totals up to date, particularly in the beginning, so as to avoid errors and ensuing conflicts which may work against the success of the system. As points are earned, lost, or spent, they should immediately be recorded in the appropriate points-earned space, points-lost space, or points-spent space. In addition, the current balance space should reflect the change so that it is always clear just how many points the child has on hand at any given time to spend on desirable outcomes.

No credit should be allowed under this sytem. The child gains access to rewards only as he earns points, and this feature keeps the child motivated to build up points

WEEKLY BEHAVIOR CHART

<u>Instructions:</u> Enter points earned, lost, and spent on the appropriate line as they are earned, lost, and spent. Keep the current balance by simply adding or subtracting as points are earned, lost, and spent. Balance remaining on Sunday night is placed into the long-term account for long-term rewards and carried over to the next week.

<u>Desirable Behaviors</u>   Point Values

1. _____   _____
   Points Earned: _____

2. _____   _____
   Points Earned: _____

3. _____   _____
   Points Earned: _____

4. _____   _____
   Points Earned: _____

5. _____   _____
   Points Earned: _____

<u>Undesirable Behaviors</u>   Point Values

1. _____   _____
   Points Lost: _____

2. _____   _____
   Points Lost: _____

3. _____   _____
   Points Lost: _____

4. _____   _____
   Points Lost: _____

5. _____   _____
   Points Lost: _____

Points Spent: _____

Current Balance: _____   L/T Account: _____

in reserve for future needs. In the event that the current balance record does fall behind somewhat, it should be possible to get the current balance at any time simply by subtracting the total of points lost and spent from the total of points earned. Under no circumstances should you neglect to record points earned, lost, and spent immediately.

Points from previous weeks which were not spent by the child by bedtime on Sunday nights go over into the long-term account; they do not carry over to the new week's short-term current balance. That fresh start each Monday, and the absence of points increases the likelihood that the child will start strongly so as to build toward the short-term desirable outcomes he knows he will want. Doing otherwise may inadvertantly encourage the child to neglect good behaviors for a while after he has accumulated a large store of short-term points. As everywhere in behavior management, consistency is important to the success of the system.

At the end of each week, look over the chart and see which behaviors have received many rewards and penalties and which have not. Such information can provide direction as you remove behaviors from the lists or change point values so as to more strongly encourage or discourage particular behaviors. These forms should be kept for several weeks or months so that you can review, if you want to, the progress that the child is making in the long run on particularly important or interesting behaviors. Such records may also dispel any controversy over, for example, long-term points accumulated several weeks previously.

As indicated, the Weekly Behavior Chart should be changed every week; indeed, it is wise to prepare several forms in advance so as to avoid confusion and delay at inconvenient times.

Current Reward Chart

The Current Reward Chart contains all of the short-term and long-term reward outcomes available within the system at any given time. Point-cost values should be listed for each reward outcome so that there is no question regarding whether the child has enough points to purchase any desirable short-term outcome and so that he knows just how many more points he will have to accumulate for a specific long-term reward. This chart may be used over several weeks, depending on changes made in available rewards and/or point values. It is good, as we've seen, to keep several rewards in effect at any one time so as to keep the child interested; it is also good to leave space for other rewards which may come up as time passes. For example, the child may want to go to a swimming meet the next evening and that may not be one of the listed reward outcomes. You may elect to charge for that activity and can do so simply by listing it as a current reward outcome. This may be particularly effective if the child is resisting doing something or persisting in some undesirable behavior. In such a case, you might more forcefully encourage appropriate behaviors by making use of a situation which you know to be strongly rewarding to the child.

Similar variations may be applied with long-term rewards, except that you must not, of course, change current point values on long-term rewards toward which the child is already working.

In this regard, you might ask the child to suggest other desirable long-term and short-term rewards and appropriate point-cost values. These suggestions that come from the child are very likely to be strongly rewarding and more likely to foster the appropriate behaviors toward which you are working.

CURRENT REWARD CHART

Instructions: Listed below are all short-term and long-term rewards which are currently being offered. Old rewards may be crossed off and new ones added as desired. Be sure child has enough points in current balance and/or long-term account to cover cost of selected rewards. Allow no credit.

Short-term Rewards   Point-Cost

1. _____   _____

2. _____   _____

3. _____   _____

4. _____   _____

5. _____   _____

6. _____   _____

7. _____   _____

8. _____   _____

9. _____   _____

10. _____   _____

Long-term Rewards   Point-Cost

1. _____   _____

2. _____   _____

3. _____   _____

4. _____   _____

5. _____   _____

Rules and Regulations

The final form suggested herein is designed to provide limitations for the operation of the home token economy. Several such limitations are indicated on the form, and space is left for entering new regulations as the need arises. It could be, for example, that one child coerces or convinces another child to "lend" him some of his points and they make an agreement. This would not be advisable for several reasons, among them the possibility that the one child is being taken advantage of and may therefore stop earning points as a means of avoiding that situation. If this does occur, it would be appropriate to list such a rule as: "You may spend only those points that *you* earn. No borrowing." With some rules, it may even be necessary to establish a point penalty for violations. This, however, will not be typical and should generally be avoided if possible.

Additional rules and regulations beyond the ones already suggested on the form can only be determined in the particular home situation. All such limitations should be reasonable and specifically designed to encourage the child to do his best in the token economy—and not to be merely restrictive for the sake of restrictions, or punitive. The child should be advised of the need for such limitations and assured that they are not just parental whims.

All three of the forms presented in this chapter, or derivatives of them, should be explained to the child when the system is introduced. In addition, it is very important that they all be posted in a public place, so that the child can refer to them at his leisure. It has been found in such home systems that the forms themselves are rewarding to the child in that they provide the structure desired and the information as to how well he is doing. Whatever forms are used, it is important that they be simple and easily understood by all concerned.

RULES AND REGULATIONS

Instructions: All rules and regulations listed below apply to everyone participating in the token economy program. Rules may be added and/or changed as the need arises. Penalties for rule violations (if any) are listed in parentheses next to the rule in question.

1. All points left over on Sunday night will automatically be placed into the long-term account. Long-term-account points may not be used for purchasing short-term rewards except under special circumstances.

2. No credit is allowed. Short-term or long-term rewards cannot be purchased without sufficient points in current balance. Debts due to loss of points must be made up before rewards can be purchased.

3. No points will be lost for undesirable behaviors not included on the list. Similarly, no points will be awarded for desirable behaviors not listed, except in the case of bonus awards.

4. _____
   _____
   _____
   _____

5. _____
   _____
   _____
   _____

Chapter 4

SPECIAL TECHNIQUES

In addition to the individual strategies for behavior management presented in Chapters 1 and 2 and the token economy program described in Chapter 3, there are several special techniques which may be used in dealing with children's behaviors. These techniques also make use of the basic principles discussed in Chapter I, and they are particularly appropriate for behavioral situations which might otherwise be especially difficult to handle.

In this chapter, the following special techniques are introduced: the behavioral contracts, behavior shaping, desensitization, time-out, response-cost, satiation, behavior anticipation, dramatization, positive avoidance, and vicarious reinforcement.

BEHAVIORAL CONTRACTS

The behavioral contract is similar in design to the token economy system except that the contract is a specific agreement, written in some detail; it may be made between parents, between children, or between parents and children. It may be, for example, that a youngster is having repeated conflicts with his older sister about her going into his room and his interrupting her telephone conversations. In this situation, it may be possible, with parental assistance, to negotiate a contract whereby each agrees to honor the other's request at the risk of some agreed-upon penalty. Such a contract may look like the one presented on the following page.

In other situations, a nagging parent and a whining child may negotiate a contract to decrease the troublesome behaviors of both. Or a yelling husband and a complaining wife may help each other to decrease behaviors which may lead to more serious conflicts as good communication breaks down. In any such situation the concerned parties make a formal commitment which is agreeable to all and which is much more likely to be upheld due to the formal structure involved and to the potential for undesirable outcomes.

When the contract is to be used, it is important that a negotiation session be held between or among the parties concerned. The idea of making an agreement involves the cooperation and voluntary commitment of all persons concerned. Negotiation allows for all persons to structure the contract in such a way that all are satisfied, increasing the likelihood of the agreement being effective without unnecessary resistance or conflict. In addition, negotiations tend to lead to better understandings of one another among family members. They provide a vehicle for communication in situations which had previously been characterized by emotional reactions and hidden hostilities.

As suggested, the contract system has utility across all age ranges. In fact, many mental health professionals report significant improvements in marital relationships when husbands and wives use the contract form to resolve some of their basic marital difficulties.

CONTRACT BETWEEN SUE AND JERRY

From this date forward or until both parties agree to cancel, the following agreement is in effect.

1. Jerry does not like Sue entering his room without his permission. If Sue does enter without such permission, she must perform all of Jerry's regular chores for that day (taking out trash, brushing dog, setting table) or, if it is late in the evening, all such chores for the following day.

2. Sue does not like Jerry interrupting her telephone conversations by getting on the extension line or by disturbing Sue directly by yelling, making noises, and the like. If Jerry does interrupt Sue in the manner indicated, Jerry must perform all of Sue's regular chores for that or the next day (clearing table, washing supper dishes, sweeping kitchen).

3. If either party fails to honor this contract, he will be penalized twenty-five cents from his weekly allowance for each occurrence.

SIGNED: _____

WITNESSED: _____

DATE: _____

BEHAVIOR SHAPING

Most human behavior is very complex, involving many small behavior parts. Take, for example, the child who does well in school. His doing well is a composite of many behaviors which lead his teachers to assess him favorably. If you wish to encourage adequate school performance in a child, particularly a child who is already experiencing difficulty, you will have to consider all the behaviors which go into adequate school performance and work on those behaviors individually and together. According to the behavioral management system, therefore, you might begin by providing desirable outcomes for doing homework, for getting involved in school-related activities, for talking about what the child is learning in the classroom, and so forth. Parental encouragement and support in such areas leads the child to become more interested and to put forth more effort.

The basic idea in behavior shaping is to start with smaller behaviors and move gradually to the larger and more complex behaviors which are seen as being desirable. Many times as the child is learning he is initially incapable of the large behaviors which the parent wishes him to demonstrate. A good example is seen in the toilet training strategy presented in Chapter 2. The child does not, all of a sudden, become trained. He must be led toward the ultimate objective.

A similar principle applies in many situations of smaller units of behavior. For example, teaching a child to have good table manners involves providing good models, rewarding for the beginning efforts to use utensils, rewarding for improvements in using utensils, and positively guiding the child as he tries increasingly difficult behaviors which go into the total impression of good table manners.

It has been emphasized repeatedly in this book that it is important to ensure success experiences for the child in the early stages of any behavior change. This emphasis embodies the shaping principle.

DESENSITIZATION

Desensitization is a procedure used by many psychologists and psychiatrists to decrease fear or anxiety in their patients. The basic procedure is a simple one which many parents may find useful, especially with a young child who tends to be fear-prone in new and potentially threatening situations. Many parents of young children express concern that their children are excessively fearful of bugs, worms, lightning and thunder, or other natural phenomena. It is most often found that such fears are created in these youngsters unknowingly by their parents who are themselves somewhat fearful and overly cautious in guiding their children in situations wherein these elements may be encountered. Taking the lightning and thunder example, many parents quickly and abruptly call their children indoors when a storm threatens. They rush about unplugging electrical applicances and closing windows and taking other precautions. As the child observes this behavior in the persons he considers to be strong and protective, he learns to be fearful and to react accordingly when other storms appear in the offing. Parents are then dismayed at the excessively fearful response that they see in the child and they tend to pay considerable attention to him so as to lessen his fear or to express their disapproval of such inappropriate behaviors as crying or hiding or whatever. This attention may then serve as an attention reward for the inappropriate behaviors and the pattern becomes more enduring.

In such a situation, where there is legitimate fearfulness, it is up to you to teach your child more appropriate behavior, that is, reasonable caution. This teaching process is desensitization, meaning allowing more comfortable and safe and reasonable feelings to dominate over the excessively fearful, threatened, and unreasonable ones. This is accomplished by providing strong parental support and strength to the child when he is in the fearful situation or at a time when he is thinking about that situation. For example, if it is raining outside, which is a mild form of a storm, it would be advisable to explain, in appropriate language, what is happening and why rain is necessary. Of course, you must yourself be confident and assured about the situation; the child will perceive your actual reactions. Sitting outside on a cloudy day might be an appropriate time to suggest that a storm might be coming and that it has a purpose and that it is not really so menacing. Sitting inside when it is stormy outside and calmly reassuring the child and demonstrating reasonable caution without fear would also be helpful. In any event, the approach involves enabling the child to become increasingly comfortable in previously fearful situations. It takes repeated efforts along these lines, with parental modeling and self-assurance being the most critical aspect. Timing is also important in attending to the child much of the time when he is not crying or hiding or demonstrating other fearful responses. In effect, the parent is decreasing the attention rewards previously only provided when the child was behaving inappropriately. If the child is already very fearful, it will take time to decrease corresponding behaviors, but the consistently confident and desensitizing parent will gradually see the effect.

Another typical situation in which fearfulness arises is with the parent who tends to be overly protective and restricting with his children. Constantly warning a child and stopping him from trying out new behaviors teaches the child to withdraw from behaving independently. Desensitization applies here in that you should demonstrate reasonable confidence in the child's ability to fend for himself at increasingly independent levels. Your presence and plainly demonstrated confidence in the child fosters confidence in himself in basically safe situations.

As he grows older, he will be able to depend increasingly and with confidence on his own capabilities.

TIME-OUT

The time-out procedure involves removing the child from a situation in which he is being rewarded for undesirable or inappropriate behaviors. The parent who sends or takes his child to his room and leaves him there for a short time when he cries is using the time-out principle. This approach has been found to be very effective in dealing with behaviors which are very difficult to ignore (provide zero outcomes) or to deal with by other means. It offers an effective alternative to scolding and spanking, which many parents come to rely on too heavily.

When a child constantly demands attention and, in the process, interrupts conversations or interferes with your performance of some task, it will be tempting to repeatedly stop what you are doing to scold the child and, after several times, to spank him. This situation may provide hidden rewards to the child in that he is gaining parental attention, even though the attention may be of a negative kind. For the child, almost any kind may be better than none at all. And so the situation continues and frequently worsens. An alternative to the scolding-spanking routine is simply to remove the child to a situation wherein he has no possibility of gaining any attention. He is placed there (such as the bedroom or bathroom) without undue fuss and directed to stay there until a few minutes after he has stopped crying or complaining. Special care must be taken to place the child into time-out calmly and to allow him to come out only after he has stopped the inappropriate behaviors. Five to fifteen minutes is usually quite sufficient.

Several parents with whom the author has worked

have developed the approach of simply telling the child to go to his room until after he has stopped crying. Typically the child stops crying rather quickly and returns to the situation where he is pleasantly greeted and attended to for non-crying behaviors.

As with all of the procedures described in this book, timing is a critical factor. The child should not be removed to the time-out area when he is not exhibiting inappropriate behaviors. For example, you should not warn the child that he will be removed from the room if he cries once more, or remove him ten minutes later after he has been quiet for a while. Only during the undesirable behavior should the child be removed. Similarly, if the child returns from time-out with a sullen and angry disposition, he should not be greeted with approval until he stops that inappropriate behavior. Otherwise, that inappropriate behavior may be inadvertantly rewarded.

RESPONSE COST

It has previously been suggested that when attempting to get a child to perform new and improved behaviors you take care not to ask for too much good performance for too little reward outcome, especially in the beginning stages of behavior change. Response cost is the reversal of that idea so as to get the child to stop seeking a specific outcome which may be desirable for him but troublesome for his parents. For example, if a child repeatedly asks for candy, or to use mother's make-up, to the point where such asking becomes annoying, and other techniques do not seem to work (such as ignoring the request), you might instead allow the child to have what he wants but only after he has completed some rather extensive and/or difficult task. In this situation, the parent may say, "OK. You may have some candy, but first I want you to sweep the kitchen and dust the furniture in the living room." When the child has completed the tasks, he is then given only a small amount of candy or whatever. It will soon become apparent to the child that the effort involved is not worth the meager reward outcome. The effect should be a significant decrease in the request for candy or other desirable outcomes except under more reasonable circumstances.

There is a real hazard in this technique: the child may come to resist doing other tasks for other outcomes also. For that reason, the response cost method should be used only sparingly and only with annoying situations which do not yield to more positive efforts.

A good variation of the response-cost method is known as the "Sunday-Box Technique." Many parents complain that their children are always leaving toys and clothing and other items lying around the house in general disarray. Some mothers say that they must constantly pick up after their children (and husbands) and always reprimand the children for being so careless. If you have this problem, it is possible quickly to eliminate it by setting up a Sunday Box. In this system, every item left in an inappropriate place is picked up by the parent and placed in a locked container which can only be opened on Sunday morning. If books, clothing, toys, or other items are not returned to their proper places after use the child (or adult!) has to do without them for the period of time between their confiscation and the next Sunday morning. No exceptions to this rule are allowed, and the child quickly learns to be careful with his belongings.

It is advisable that parents also be subject to the rule so that the child feels that what is appropriate for him is also appropriate for everyone else in the home. Parents may even go out of their way occasionally to "accidentally" leave something out that the child can confiscate. A good-natured game approach appears to work best— but the rules of the game are held firm and consistent.

SATIATION

Many people like ice cream or like going for walks or like to watch television, but too much of anything can become unpleasant and undesirable. Satiation is the technique of giving the child something he wants in such excess that he tends to want it less or not at all. The author had occasion to discuss a situation with a mother whose little boy would eat little more than mashed potatoes at suppertime. No matter how she and her husband tried to encourage the boy to eat other foods, he resisted and, as a result, would be hungry later and request snacks before bedtime. In this situation the boy was getting so much attention for eating just potatoes, and not really starving as a result, that he persisted. It was suggested to this mother that at suppertime she give everyone else the regular portions of food, but that for the boy she just provide a plate full of mashed potatoes, nothing more. No attention was directed at the boy and he was permitted to eat potatoes to his heart's content. Later in the evening when he requested snacks, he was given warmed potatoes and nothing else. The satiation procedure continued until the boy *requested* some other foods for supper. The request was warmly responded to and as he ate other foods he was praised for being a good eater and so forth. Satiation, then, is the excessive use of a desirable outcome until that outcome becomes less desirable.

BEHAVIOR ANTICIPATION

Behavior anticipation means simply observing when conflicts tend to arise and structuring situations so that the typical problems are avoided. This is particularly appropriate when there are two or more children in the family who tend to argue with one another over minor things such as who gets to ride in the front seat of the car, who gets the last piece of pie, and who should take his bath first. These situations can be avoided quite easily by not allowing any children to ride up front, by cutting the pie so that none is left or not putting what is left on the table, and by calling each child individually for his bath rather than announcing generally that it is "bath time." Of course, minor conflicts between and among children will happen regardless of what you do; they are necessary for the children to learn how to get along with each other and with people in general. Such altercations become problems only when they upset the rest of the family and foster additional conflicts which may lead to more serious difficulties. It is the wise parent who anticipates some of these trouble spots and facilitates good interpersonal relationships among family members. Too often the parent becomes the judge or referee in minor conflict situations and the children learn to control parents' attention by staging such useful fights. When the inevitable fights do occur, it is best to allow, as much as possible, for the children's own resolution of the problem. If you must get involved, it is best not to take sides. An example of this is seen in the situation where two children are arguing over a toy. Rather than enter the situation and decide whose toy it is, and then scold one and give the toy to the other, it would be better to remove the toy calmly. Both children learn that fighting over toys results in the loss of the toy regardless of what the situation might be. In this way, the children learn to resolve their differences without loud and aggressive conflicts.

DRAMATIZATION

Many times a child has difficulty in performing a certain behavior because he has not had occasion to perform such behaviors in the past. He may, then, be inclined to return to old and often inappropriate behavior patterns when placed in a new situation. One such example is seen in the child who visits a friend of mother's who has a child of approximately the same age as the youngster. Many times the two children will play together, and the visiting child may try to take over toys or situations. The task, of course, is to teach the child appropriate guest behaviors so that he does not offend his hosts and, perhaps, interfere with the adult relationship. In such a situation you might prepare the child for visiting by making believe with him that you are playing together as the child will be with his new friend. In the process of such pretending, you can comment upon and provide desirable outcomes for socially appropriate behaviors. Similarly, when the child is actually in the situation and later, after you have returned home, the child may be praised for conducting himself appropriately and in line with the practice behaviors of dramatization. Children enjoy such dramatization and they tend to respond well to parental attention in this play situation. The usefulness of this approach extends to several similar situations.

Another example is the preparation of the child for going out to a restaurant. Dinner time can be turned into such a dramatization session with younger children by suggesting that all pretend that they are sitting in a "famous" restaurant and behaving appropriately. Again, rewarding outcomes for such approximations of desirable behaviors should work well, and you can remind the child of such practice sessions when the family is actually in a restaurant. This technique provides the child with a structure for behaving and he can more effectively predict what the outcomes are likely to be.

Beyond these preparation examples, dramatization can be used to intervene in typical conflict situations between siblings. If two children have become involved in minor skirmishes about such minor matters as discussed above, you may suggest that they practice getting along better under parent supervision. The children could actually go through one of their little spats and be counseled on the inappropriateness of it as it develops. Care should be taken in these instances not to hold such practice sessions during or immediately following an actual altercation because the children may learn that fighting will bring the attention of the concerned parent. Waiting for a peaceful and cooperative time should work better in getting the children to benefit from such practical instruction and related desirable outcomes.

Positive Avoidance

This technique is very similar to the time-out approach discussed above except that instead of removing the child from the situation, you remove yourself. The effect tends to be essentially the same. Some mental health professionals suggest that the parent retreat to the bathroom when a temper tantrum or some other attention-seeking behavior is in the making. That way the child loses the possibility of gaining the desired outcome (attention) and the possibility only returns as he returns to a more reasonable disposition. The difficulty with this, as with other zero-outcome techniques, is that the child's first reaction is to behave more excessively in an effort to force the parent to return his attention. For example, the child who throws a temper tantrum may, upon parent departure, try really drastic measures such as breaking objects or screaming near-obscenities. Many parents tend to give in at that point and return to the child to punish or scold him for such excess. In effect, the parent who returns at that point teaches the child that only excessively unreasonable behaviors will work in gaining his objectives and the parent can expect more of the same. Therefore, if at all possible, you should resist returning until the child has stopped the negative behaviors, teaching him thereby that only appropriate behaviors will result in attention and that inappropriate behaviors are useless. If the child's safety is endangered or he is doing something that absolutely cannot be tolerated, you should return, calmly punish without comment, and again return to the place of avoidance. If you can get past such situations in this manner the first few times, chances are that that behavior will diminish as the child learns that his efforts are not worth the undesirable outcomes. Of course, the more desirable behaviors should be heavily attended to and rewarded so that the child learns more effective and appropriate means of gaining his desired outcomes.

Vicarious Reinforcement

All people learn a great deal by observing what others get for what they do. The toddler who witnesses his little friend get spanked for running into the street is less likely to run into the street himself for fear of the same outcome. Similarly, children learn to imitate the behaviors of others which appear to lead to desirable outcomes. The parent who is aware of this can indirectly teach one child to behave in a particular manner by rewarding another child in his presence for behaving in that manner. In addition, you can very effectively teach by exhibiting the behavior yourself; all children tend to emulate the behaviors of their parents.

An example of vicarious reinforcement is seen in the situation where six-year-old Tommy is reinforced or rewarded for having washed his hands so well and four-year-old Timmy is given no instructions about his hands. Timmy learns by observation that good handwashing leads to desirable outcomes. When Timmy later washes his hands and receives a similar reaction from his parents, he is being rewarded both for handwashing and for imitating an appropriate behavior.

Children are surrounded by models, both appropriate and inappropriate. The wise parent selects and regulates available models for his children with reasonable caution. Research indicates that television and other media, in addition to live models, can have both positive and negative influences on the behaviors of children. Television in particular, since it is so easily accessible to the child, should be monitored with the potential impact of models and vicarious reinforcement kept in mind.

Chapter 5

THE BEHAVIORAL ATTITUDE

Attitude is defined as a feeling or disposition or orientation toward persons or situations. Your attitude system directs your actions and gives consistency to your behavioral tendencies. If you have a behavioral attitude, that behavioral orientation will give structure to your actions and such actions will be consistent with, and as effective as, the behavioral management scheme presented in this book. It has been said in this book that a noted advantage of the behavioral management system is that it enables the parent, perhaps for the first time, to have confidence in a consistent system by which he can deal with the constantly changing and challenging aspects of parenthood. This is a critical aspect of the child-rearing process, in that inconsistency and related behavioral extremes contribute heavily to maladjustment in children and conflict in the total family.

A mental health professional once told me that in working with parents his objectives are to get them to talk differently, to behave differently, and finally to talk and behave similarly. The first objective, to talk differently, relates to this book's aim to teach you to understand and translate situations in terms of the behavioral management principles presented in this book. The second objective, to behave differently, relates to the actual implementation of the behavioral principles with children and others. Finally, the last objective, to talk and behave similarly, suggests that once you understand the behavioral management principles and have tried them out in your own life, then you can incorporate the strategies into your home situation and behave and think with consistency and effectiveness.

In order to develop a behavioral attitude, you must know that appropriate principles well enough to apply them across a wide variety of situations, involving not only the behaviors of children but also behaviors of yourself and other adults in your life experience. Effective applications of behavior principles are based on several important concepts which have been dealt with at varying length throughout this book and which are summarized below for additional clarification.

BEHAVIOR AND PERSONALITY

Behavior is what people do; the consistency of their behavior in discernible patterns is what others see as their personalities. While the development of personality is dependent upon the manifestation over time of specific behaviors, there is a common and unfortunate, tendency among many people to assign significance to behaviors based on shakily-founded assumptions about personality —that is, without adequate behavioral observation. All too often labels are attached to people who do not have all of the characteristics that the label is meant to cover. The fact that many people are mis-labeled due to the critical inadequacy of labelling systems is bad enough, but that labels do not lead to effective management of problem behavior is the more immediate concern. The parent who contacts the behavior specialist about his son's strange behavior is certain to be asked to specify what he means by "strange." Little if anything can be done to deal with a general class of behavior until the specific behavioral elements are known. The behavioral specialist—and the behavioral parent—become effective in managing behavior by looking at it for what it is. That is: in terms of outcomes, what purpose does that particular behavior have? Only when the specific outcomes of specific and observable behaviors are known can a corrective procedure of outcome manipulation be implemented. The behavioral parent must take care to look at behavior in terms of what the child or other person actually *does.* Changes in personality follow changes in behavior.

BEHAVIOR MODIFICATION

Since behaviors are influenced by their outcomes, it follows that modification of those behaviors by parents and others is dependent upon the extent to which they have control of the outcomes involved. The younger the child, the more dependent he is upon his parents for need and wish fulfillment. As he grows older and his relationships extend to other persons, particularly his peer group, he becomes less dependent upon his parents and thus less controllable by them. Since this is the case, the earlier the parent can establish effective influence and appropriate behavior patterns, the more his influence will remain effective as the child becomes, in fact, more independent. If the young child is forced to comply with parental wishes, he will become less compliant as the forcefulness deteriorates. The parents of a rebellious adolescent will wonder why their youngster does not listen to them; never realizing that he does not have to listen to meet his needs, and that his listening itself has never been made desirable by effective parental management of desirable outcomes for desirable behaviors.

ASSOCIATION AND AVOIDANCE

Continuing parental influence as the child grows older is maintained by the child's association of desirable consequences with socially appropriate behaviors. If the parent is seen by the child as desirable because of his association with desirable outcomes, then the child will choose to continue the association by continuing to comply with parental directives. If the parent is seen by the child as undesirable because of his association with a preponderance of undesirable outcomes, then the child will choose to avoid the parent and resist his directives as such resistance becomes more effective. From the beginning, the parent is building associations in the child, and the more positively oriented parent is establishing greater and more enduring influence as the child grows older. This is a particularly important consideration for the parent who characteristically threatens the child in order to gain appropriate behaviors. The child who complies with parental demands primarily as a means of avoiding undesirable outcomes, as opposed to complying to gain desirable outcomes, is bound, as time and growth permits, to avoid the threatening parent and to defy the behavioral patterns associated with that parent.

THE SOURCE

It follows from what is suggested above that the source for change in children's behaviors and, correspondingly, their personalities is to be found in the changes made by persons controlling the outcomes that children receive. Children will change only to the extent that their outcomes are modified; that is, only to the extent that their parents and other significant persons in their lives change the management of their outcomes. A parent cannot send his child to a specialist and expect that the specialist will somehow influence the child, without giving the specialist significant control over the child's outcomes over an extended period of time. In fact, the specialist changes the behaviors of parents and only indirectly, through them, the behaviors of their children. Ultimately, then, any change in children means change in their parents and, perhaps, in others with significant influence. In view of this, it remains for the parent *first* to manage his own behavior effectively in order to manage effectively the behavior of his children.

SELF-MANAGEMENT

In changing his own behavior the parent has two starting points, suggested at the beginning of this chapter. First, he may begin to talk differently, leading to behaving differently. Second, he may begin to behave differently, leading to corresponding changes in talking.

Talking Differently

A persons's attitude is assessed partially by what he says, and an attitude determines how a person will behave under given circumstances—such as managing children's behavior. A primary way of influencing a person's attitude, then, is to influence his talking. And since talking is behavior, it is subject to influence through outcomes just as any other behavior is. Therefore, the influence of talking is accomplished by providing desirable outcomes for appropriate talking and by providing zero or undesirable outcomes for inappropriate talking. The parent who is concerned with changing his talking as a starting point is in control of many of his own outcomes and, therefore, he is in a position to influence his own talking behavior toward what he comes to know to be desirable talking behavior. Reading this book and listening to behavior specialists are ways of learning what appropriate talking is and now you should be ready to approve (provide desirable outcomes) or disapprove (provide undesirable outcomes) of your own talking behavior.

Appropriate talking involves shifting the emphasis toward the positive interpretations of situations, seeing the desirable elements, and the potential for change, in every situation. Many parents who are less effective in managing their own behaviors and the behaviors of their children spend a disproportionate amount of time and energy in complaining about the circumstances and in looking for ways to explain away their own inadequacies and those of their children. This compensatory talk only serves temporarily to relieve feelings of guilt and inadequacy. In the long run it perpetuates ineffective behaviors. If you want to make constructive changes in your own behaviors, leading to corresponding changes in those around you, you might begin by making a concerted effort to be aware of what you say and why, or what the outcomes for your talking may be. Once you have done this, by applying your knowledge of behavioral outcomes you should be able to acquire the same or similar outcomes through more nearly appropriate and effective behaviors.

The specific instances wherein positive talking can be instituted are just about infinite in number and variety. The key is to select the positive aspects of any situation for comment so as to build positive associations, create positive expectations, and construct positive attitudes. For example, when the child comes home from school with a test on which half of the items are marked incorrect, the parent may comment on half being correct, thereby rewarding the child for what he has accomplished and increasing the likelihood of continued improvement for desirable outcomes. A negative comment may only teach the child not to bring papers home, so as to avoid the negative outcome, or that inappropriate performance results in attention, potentially a desirable outcome in this situation. More importantly, as you talk positively you come to develop a more positive attitude which will increase more positive behaviors across various other situations.

Behaving Differently

The other possible starting point is simply to begin to assert yourself in a positive manner; this can result in more positive outcomes and corresponding changes in talking. Success breeds success, and as you become more successful in managing behaviors with systematic efforts, you tend to develop greater confidence with corresponding attitudes and feelings. The circular nature of the whole process should be apparent. With concerted effort in behaving differently, meaning in coordination with good management principles, you should either talk less, or talk in the more positive manner suggested above. The combination of the two is, of course, to be preferred, and that combination is the ultimate behavioral attitude.

As an example, the parent who intends to behave differently would at the start take care to provide desirable outcomes immediately after the child has accomplished some desirable objective or even a reasonable approximation of one. In conjunction with such effort, the parent would provide zero or undesirable outcomes following behaviors which are the opposites or contradictions of the desirable alternatives. You might, for example, attend liberally to a child when he is not interrupting adult conversations and ignore or utilize time-out procedures when the child does interrupt. This powerful approach should lead to an increase in desirable behaviors and a decrease in the undesirable alternative, resulting eventually in a more positive perception of and attitude toward the child and related situations.

Combinations

As you become more consistent and effective in your combinations of efforts to change behaviors and talking in yourself, resulting in corresponding changes in the behaviors of your children, you will come increasingly to view a greater number of situations from a behavioral viewpoint. As this viewpoint becomes functional, it can be said that the behavioral attitude has been developed. The cost to you of the total change is time, concerted effort in controlling your own behaviors, and consistency engendered by the systematic nature of the behavioral management system.

Chapter 6

SELF-MODIFICATION

Underlying the possibility of managing or changing your children's behaviors toward more desirable levels is the need for effective management and modification of your own behaviors. The behavioral attitude, discussed in the preceding chapter, is a general orientation to making yourself more effective as a parent. In this chapter you are encouraged to take a closer look at your behaviors, and you are provided with specific guidelines for self-modification. This area of personal growth is receiving increasing attention from specialists in mental health fields, and references for detailed discussions of self-management are included at the end of this book.

Steps to Self–Control

The ability to positively influence the behaviors of others, especially children, is closely related to the ability to effectively manage your own behavior. Research in education and psychology consistently reveals that the effective teacher and the effective parent are appropriately described as effective persons, meaning persons who are self-directed and caring. Such self-direction is not an accident; it is the product of good management of one's own outcomes and goals. Many parents are fortunate in having had effective teachers (parents) who started them early on the road toward positive self-control. Many have not been so fortunate.

Self-control involves, first, a knowledge of how you learn to behave in particular ways. Having read the preceding chapters, you now understand that behavior is outcome-directed. To put it simply, you do what you do because of what you get for what you do. If you can identify what you want and attach it to what you do, you can change your behaviors very effectively. All of the principles presented thus far for effecting change in your children's behaviors apply to self-modification. Rather than reintroducing those concepts, the steps to self-control are presented with the general assumption that the underlying principles are recognized and understood.

STEP 1.   Choose a single behavior of your own that you would like to change and describe it (write it down) in terms of what you actually do. Be specific, and keep it simple. If you are concerned about always putting things off, specify one thing that you put off that seems to lead to other problems. You may not, for example, do the dishes right after the meal is ended, and that may lead to interference and stress as other tasks come due. Such stress interferes with anyone's ability to be calm and controlled in dealing with others, especially children. The behavior you are concerned about, then, may be expressed in terms of "not doing the dishes within a reasonable time after the meal is concluded." Such a specific expression sets the stage for the next step in the self-modification sequence.

STEP 2.   At this point you are ready to decide and specify what you want to accomplish—your behavioral goal. In the example provided, it is apparent that your intention is to do the dishes within a reasonable time after the meal is completed. It only remains to define what is meant by a reasonable time. Let's say that you decide that thirty minutes is reasonable. Your behavioral goal, then, is to wash the dishes used for any meal within thirty minutes after completion of that meal. You may even go further by specifying that the end of the meal is understood to be marked by everyone's having left the table.

STEP 3.   When you know what behavior you have and what behavior you wish to accomplish, you are ready to look for outcomes that can be connected to the behaviors in question in order to effect the change. What you are really doing here is identifying those things you want or want to do which can be withheld until you perform the behavior in question. In this situation, let's say that you like dessert or you like to smoke a cigarette at the end of a meal. Since you like or want those experiences, you can use them to reward yourself for behavior changes or restrict them for failures to change. There are, of course, many other such outcomes that you could use, but we will use these to exemplify the procedure.

STEP 4.   You are now ready to make a behavior-change contract with yourself utilizing the elements provided in the preceding steps. You may, if you wish, make an informal contract or understanding with yourself, but it is generally advisable to make a formal and quite specific agreement so that you are less inclined to cheat or simply forget the whole thing. In such a contract you should specify your behavioral goal and precisely what leads to what. Your contract in the situation suggested might read something like this: "My objective is to begin doing the dishes within thirty minutes after everyone leaves the table at each of the three daily meals. On each occasion that I meet this requirement, I shall be entitled to smoke one cigarette or substitute another desirable activity upon completion of the dishes. When I do not meet the requirement, I shall not allow myself to smoke the cigarette or substitute another desirable activity for a minimum of one hour."

Making such a contract with yourself leaves little doubt as to what you wish and intend to do. You may think it a little strange when you go through this process for the first time, but such a structured approach has been repeatedly proven effective in getting people started in making desired changes. Without it, the tendency is to make halfhearted attempts that typically end in failure. From the behavioral viewpoint, you can readily see that giving up on halfhearted attempts enables you to escape an undesirable activity. Such escape acts as a reward for giving up! With this in mind, it is little wonder that people who try to change without specific and firm resolve fail repeatedly. Such individuals might be described as having little "willpower," but the fact is that they have unwittingly rewarded themselves for giving up in the past. Remember: reward for a behavior increases the likelihood of recurrence of that behavior.

STEP 5.   Stick with it. Early in the change process it will probably be difficult to follow through with your plan. However, with each occasion of meeting your contract it will become easier to comply. Eventually it will become automatic, because the situation will prompt the behavior and the reward will have made the behavior durable and, perhaps, desirable—or, at least, less undesirable.

STEP 6.   Once the behavior is consistent and no longer a source of conflict, you should be aware of the intrinsically rewarding aspect of having exerted effective control over your own behaviors. You will have been rewarded for perseverance, and you will, correspondingly, be stronger in subsequent efforts to alter and strengthen other behaviors. You are then in a position to make another contract for another change. With each succeeding contract you will become better controlled, or more self-disciplined and better prepared to regulate your management behaviors in relation to your children. Such an attitude of confidence, or its absence, is readily perceived by children, and they tend to react accordingly.

Techniques for Self–Management

In the preceding section you are provided with a systematic plan for progressively changing behaviors toward a more desirable level of self-control. In fact there are many more things that you can do to increase the effectiveness of your efforts, depending on how aware you become of those elements in your experience that exert influence over what you do. In this section we will consider several additional techniques that should enable you to increase the possibility of managing your own behaviors more effectively. All of the procedures presented below have been utilized by mental health professionals in enabling people they help to become more positively self-directed.

Self-Reward and Self-Punishment

Self-reward and self-punishment are probably the most widely used techniques for getting individuals to change their undesirable patterns of behavior. In this approach you are encouraged to use a plan similar to the one presented above wherein you determine what changes you want to make and what outcomes, desirable and undesirable, you can and will use. In this approach you must be careful to select those outcomes that you strongly desire or really wish to avoid. There are any number of possibilities, depending on your personal likes and dislikes.

A few years ago I counseled a young mother who described her problem as one of always yelling at her children. After we had carefully defined the behavior in question and specified the reasonable goal she desired, we set up a program of self-reward and self-punishment designed to reduce such yelling and to increase more positive parent-child interactions. Briefly, the plan included having the mother record each time she yelled at her kids and having her total the number of such incidents at 8 P.M. each day. At that time, if she had yelled three or fewer times (her initial goal), she would allow herself to watch television (a very desirable outcome) for three hours. If the yelling incidents exceeded three, she penalized herself by reducing her television-watching time by thirty minutes per incident. After she had reduced her yelling consistently to three or less, we reduced the allowable frequency to two, and so on. Once the yelling stopped we reversed the procedure by putting her in a position to "earn" her television-viewing time by means of attending to her children's good behaviors. That is, each time she initiated positive attention toward her children for some desirable behavior—which she had done only infrequently in the past—she added fifteen minutes to her desirable outcome.

This young woman had tried unsuccessfully to control her tendency to yell too much many times prior to starting the program. Before she succeeded she very often remarked, "Well, my mother yelled at us kids a lot and

I guess that's why I am the way I am." No doubt your parents have a significant influence on how you behave as adults, but the possibilities of self-modification through systematically applied learning principles can help you to avoid the same mistakes in teaching your children.

The possible variations of self-reward and self-punishment are limitless. I recently heard of a situation wherein a young man was troubled by his unreasonable desire to check and recheck the security of his home after he had gone to bed. Every night after retiring he would begin to think about whether or not the doors had been locked, the windows closed, the lights turned out, the appliances turned off, and so forth. On many nights he would get up, go downstairs, and check in great detail every possible source of hazard. On some nights he would go through the same ritual two or three times. He knew he was being unreasonable, but he could not get the idea out of his mind and could not sleep until he had acted upon his impulse.

The self-management technique suggested to him by a local mental health counselor proved very effective in getting rid of that troublesome behavior. He was instructed to continue to act on his impulse to check the house but to add two new dimensions. First, after getting out of bed and before going downstairs, he was required to sit down at his desk and list every item he intended to check in his survey of the house. He was then to proceed with going through the ritual. Secondly, when he returned to his room he was required again to sit down at his desk and to list everything he had checked and, in addition, to write one paragraph on how he felt about having gone through the sequence. He was instructed that there was to be no exception to this plan. However, if he did not choose to go through the ritual, he was not required to do anything.

If you think about this self-management approach, you can readily see what should—and did—happen. The young man retired at about 11 P.M. and it was typically 11:30 P.M. or so by the time he decided to check the house. The checking behavior itself took about twenty minutes. When he required himself to sit down at his desk before and after the ritual was performed, he was adding, usually, another thirty to forty minutes to the whole incident. The troublesome behavior was costing him as much as one or two hours. With these conditions in effect, he quickly concluded that checking the house was just not worth the time and trouble. This response-cost approach to self-management has repeatedly been shown to be effective in changing behavior patterns. As you can see in the example given, the individual is punishing himself (spending additional time) for performing the undesirable behavior *and* rewarding himself (avoiding the expenditure of time) for not performing the troublesome ritual.

We all use or experience these self-reward and self-punishment techniques frequently in our everyday lives: if you do your work now, you won't have to do it later and vice versa; if you have a helping of potatoes, you may not have dessert; if you buy a new car, you cannot afford new carpeting; if you don't smoke cigarettes, you will feel better; and so forth. The important point about using these techniques effectively is that they are used systematically and in line with an improved understanding of the complex nature of human behavior. The better and the sooner you can see the outcomes of your various behaviors, the more effective those outcomes will be in influencing your behaviors.

The single largest problem in using self-reward and self-punishment techniques is that it is very often too easy for you to fail to follow through with the plan. Many people drift into making exceptions and putting off outcomes. Later they wonder why the procedure did not work. As mentioned above, putting something off or making exceptions to the plan involves rewarding undesirable behaviors. It is sometimes helpful to involve someone else who can help you to control your early inclinations to give up. Many times, just telling your spouse or a friend about your efforts will keep you on track. Encouraging such people to provide desirable and undesirable outcomes themselves can be effective. Going to a counselor for support and direction in the early stages is often a good idea. The more specific the plan and the more support available, especially in the early going, the better the chances for success.

In addition to the basic outcome management strategies, several other techniques can be utilized to strengthen change efforts. Those that follow can be used alone or, preferably, in combination with one another or in combination with outcome management.

Self-Observation

A very simple technique that has been found to be surprisingly effective involves looking at your own behaviors. Very often people are not really sufficiently aware of what they are doing or of what the impact of their behaviors is. We all know that we learn to alter our behaviors in interpersonal settings according to what others tell us, directly or indirectly, about ourselves. You can add significantly to personal awareness—and change —by keeping track of how you behave in a variety of situations. Self-observation means measuring the occurrence of important behaviors in a variety of situations. In the example given above of the young mother who yelled excessively at her children, it is likely that just keeping track of yelling helped her to be more aware of and controlled in such situations. Several studies have confirmed that this approach does, in fact, work. For example, heavy smokers have been found to reduce their smoking behavior when they decided to record each cigarette smoked; passive and submissive individuals have been found to become more assertive when they kept track of both passive and assertive behaviors; parents have increased their consistency in responding to their children by identifying their inconsistencies and recording them. Exactly why these changes occur in most situations is not yet clear to researchers, but the fact is that they do occur.

Self-observation typically is used in combination with other change strategies, and it is probably most efficient when used in that fashion. However, the technique can yield very positive results by itself. The procedure consists of simply identifying the behavior, positive or negative, that you are concerned about and deciding upon some means of record keeping. Usually, just counting the behavior is sufficient; but you may wish to describe it or measure how long it lasts, or whatever. The more effort you put into it, the better the end result.

Situation Control

Another very effective and common-sense technique involves identifying the situations in which behaviors occur and stopping the occurrence of those behaviors in those situations. That is, your objective is not to stop the behaviors totally but to restrict their occurrence to a limited number of settings.

People come to associate certain behaviors with specific situations. Those situations then become prompts or cues for the occurrence of the associated behaviors. Think for a minute about snacking behaviors, which, for many, result in undesirable weight gain. Eating behavior is powerfully reinforced by the satisfaction of a basic biological need. We all like to and must eat. If, after a period of time, you have begun to eat in settings (in front of the television) other than those usually associated with eating (the dining table), the long-term effect is to eat more frequently. You may discover that eating in those situations occurs even though you are not actually hungry. That is a common and, sometimes, surprising discovery.

Situation control involves (1) destroying the associations between the situations and the undesirable behaviors and (2) building associations by performing desirable behaviors in those situations in which you want them to occur. There are many possible applications of this effective procedure.

In the case of undesirable snacking behaviors, the approach would be to restrict eating to only the dining table. When you get the urge to snack as you are sitting in front of the television, your response would be to prepare the snack and to consume it at the table, not in front of the television. In any situation where your impulse is to snack, you must go to the table, and there you should do nothing else but eat. Don't read the paper, don't listen to music, don't socialize, and so forth. In time the tendency or impulse to eat in other situations will diminish, and you will decrease your snacking behaviors. It works. I have counseled several people who have lost considerable weight by following through on this simple approach.

The same idea can be applied to other troublesome behaviors, and it can be very useful in building in new, more constructive behavior patterns. I once worked with a young man, a college student, who had considerable difficulty in studying and, as a result, was doing very poorly in school. In his apartment he had available to him a quiet place where he could go and study whenever he wished. Every time he got into that situation, however, he found himself drinking coffee and daydreaming and, eventually, leaving to do something more enjoyable. According to him, he just could not concentrate; he couldn't get started. It seemed that something was always happening to interfere with what he was supposed to be doing. When we looked at the situation, it became clear that he had come to associate various nonstudying behaviors with that setting. Whenever he sat down and tried to work, he would experience impulses to do a variety of things—get coffee, leaf through an available magazine, think about his girl friend, and so on. When he did try to concentrate, he couldn't. Finally he would simply give up and, in effect, reward giving up by escaping the difficult task of studying.

The plan for alleviating this problem was very simple and, as it turned out, quite effective. First, it was decided that he should select a time period during which it was unlikely that he would be disturbed for any reason. He selected 3 P.M. to 6 P.M. as the best possible time within his daily routines. He was advised that at 3 P.M. every day he was to go to his study area and begin reading his assignments. He was not to go to that area at any other time except to read school-related materials. Under no circumstances was he to go to that area except to perform studying behaviors—no letter writing, no leisure reading, no eating. Once there, if he had difficulty studying he was directed to read one page and then leave. After several minutes or an hour he was to return to the study area and, again, try to concentrate. If he still had difficulty, he was directed to read one more page and leave again. He followed through on this plan for several days, and then the requirement prior to leaving was increased to two pages. Over a period of seven weeks, he had increased the requirement to ten pages per sitting. With this gradual increase of studying it became easier to concentrate for the prearranged activity period. Importantly, he was to stay in that situation only as long as he studied. The earlier associations of daydreaming and so forth had been lost because they were no longer occurring in that situation. As the associations were lost, new associations of studying were being established and studying became automatic, being prompted by the situation. In addition a consistent time each day became associated with studying behavior, and he didn't schedule other activities which had, in the past, interfered.

Everyone establishes some kinds of routines in his life in order to regulate his behaviors. As a parent, you can recognize very well the importance of routines in managing children's behaviors. Children respond most cooperatively to parental requirements when they know what to expect and when to expect it. Similarly, you can be most efficient and self-directed when you regulate your situations and their corresponding associations. If you are not reasonably organized and consistent in the performance of your duties, you probably have difficulty in keeping up with your responsibilities. That personal ineffectiveness can, and very often does, lead to confusion and anxiety. Being in such a state makes you vulnerable to pressures from your spouse and your children, resulting in emotional reactions and poor behavior management efforts.

Like all other self-management approaches, situation control should be gradually introduced. Demanding too much change in the early stages increases the likelihood of failure. Start by identifying one situation and getting the appropriate behaviors regulated therein. You might be surprised to find that just that first change will yield positive results across several other situations. That is the usual result of such self-management efforts—success breeds success. It is usually best to select the behavior that is most troublesome; it is possibly the indirect source of several other related difficulties. Regardless of the specific behavior-situation area you might choose to regulate, the same principles of situation control apply.

Underlying this approach is the notion that we often learn to associate behaviors, places, people, and feelings that occur together. This is an extremely important idea as we look at all aspects of child- and self-management. Like parents, children come to associate various feelings, behaviors, and expectations with parents, siblings, teachers, classrooms, homes, and so forth. If a child sees his parent as typically reacting to him with criticism and punishment, he comes to associate that parent with undesirable feelings. As growth and development allow, he will tend to avoid or ignore that parent in order to escape those feelings. In that situation, it is not surprising that the child will tune out his parents and resist controls. The older and more independent the child becomes, the more capable he is in rendering the parent ineffective. On the other hand, the parent who establishes positive associations with his children has a growing capability for influencing his child to cooperate and for keeping the channels of communication open. Maintaining good self-control and implementing positive management procedures tremendously enhances the successfulness of rearing children.

As with other techniques, situation control has broad applications in your everyday life, both in managing your own and your children's behaviors. If you consider the associations people make, you will realize that there are many situations in which you do particular things that are precipitated by those situations. If you typically smoke after you eat, you experience the urge to smoke when you finish eating. If you routinely do the wash every Monday morning, you will experience some uneasiness on that Monday morning when you cannot, for some reason, do the wash. It is that uneasiness, that expectation of doing something, that sets the stage for behaving in particular ways. It is also that uneasiness—which we often call "anxiety"—that makes it difficult to change our habits or routines. We escape the anxiety by performing the behaviors associated with given situations. Good self-management means that you learn to tolerate the uneasiness as you set up new expectations for more desirable behaviors.

Like yourself, your children use their expectations to regulate their behaviors in meeting their needs. Because they are younger and more dependent on the adults around them to fulfill their needs, the adults are in a powerful position to make desirable behaviors in appropriate situations work best for the child as he gains his desired outcomes. In other words, parents train their children to expect to meet their needs satisfactorily through good behavior. Situation control is an important part of that complex process.

Thought Control

You probably have not very often seen adults around you talking to themselves. You might consider it to be strange behavior. But, in fact, people are constantly talking to themselves, even you. We all think in language, and much of thinking is really subvocal self-talk. In children we see self-talk, we expect it, and we tolerate it because youngsters are not yet socialized and not subjected to the same restraints as are adults.

The fact that we see such behavior in children and recognize it in ourselves has important implications for how we behave and for the possibilities of changing our own behaviors. Since we think (self-talk) about what we are going to do and what we have done, it is clear that what we "say" has a direct bearing on what we do. One avenue of changing what we do, then, is through modifying what we say.

At the extremes of inappropriate behavior, seriously mentally ill persons have been taught to talk to themselves in terms of how they should and should not behave. "Be calm." "Keep it relevant." "Don't get bizarre." These are typical self-instructions encouraged in psychotic individuals as they are about to interact with others. The findings from studies utilizing nonpsychotic self-talk have been favorable, yielding behavior changes that approach more closely the desirable levels of normalcy. These psychotic individuals are trained to give themselves instructions, comment on their behaviors, and verbally practice or rehearse interactions which, in the past, had resulted in inappropriate behaviors. These patients are even encouraged to praise themselves after they have succeeded in behaving in particular ways.

We all talk ourselves out of and into certain actions; we rationalize, and intellectualize, and so on. The point of effective thought control is that we force ourselves to talk differently—more positively. One such technique is "thought stopping." If you find yourself getting depressed and upset because of some mistake you made in reacting to your children or anyone else in your experience, your bad feelings are probably accompanied and worsened by repeated self-criticisms. Such self-blame heightens anxiety and sets the stage for more mistakes in the future. Bad feelings cause us to focus on ourselves and to utilize our energies to make ourselves feel better. With the expenditure of energy and attention in that manner, there is a diminished capability of dealing reasonably with external situations. The outcome is usually poor judgment, undesirable results, more self-criticism, heightened anxiety, and so on. Thought stopping involves simply shutting off the excessive self-criticism by saying to yourself, "Stop!" Say it to yourself with emphasis and, at that point, do in fact stop the negative thoughts. In the early going the thought may soon begin again, but if you practice the self-instruction repeatedly, stopping each time, it will not be long before you can control those thoughts for extended periods. As they come under control, your corresponding behaviors will improve and a positive thinking-behaving cycle will have begun.

Another very effective variation of thought control is "behavior rehearsal." As the name suggests, this technique involves talking yourself through the situation several times before it is actually encountered. Unfortunately, the tendency of many people who are afraid of some situation is either not to think about it or to think about it in terms of the likelihood of their behaving poorly in it. This is especially true of individuals who tend to be passive and easily intimidated in relation to more aggressive and domineering people. The fact that they behave in that manner in anticipation of the feared situation is not too surprising. The person who does not think about it is avoiding the stress associated with the situation, and the one who expects to do poorly is stressed less when he does actually do poorly. Thinking constructively, on the other hand, increases the likelihood that those more desirable (effective) behaviors will occur in that situation. This leads to more success (desirable outcomes), which increases the chance of recurrence of such behaviors in similar situations.

In short, thought control means to regulate your self-talk in such a way that you stop thoughts that contradict your strengths and you use thoughts that reinforce those strengths. Like many other techniques presented in this book, thought control may appear artificial or unnatural at first—and it is. You are attempting to break away from what has become natural for you because you are suffering as a result of those tendencies. Changing, making the unnatural natural, is difficult for everyone, and these techniques of self-control can only point the direction and ease the process for you. Whether you change or not is up to you; if you think you can, the odds are in your favor.

Internal Stress Control

We all experience anxiety and tension, and we learn to associate these states of internal stress with a variety of circumstances and experiences in our lives. Unfortunately, too often these feelings interfere with our ability to function effectively in those everyday situations. Fear of speaking in front of a group, for example, may lead to poor performance or to attempts to avoid that situation altogether. The latter tendency in such situations is the more serious of the two, because avoiding doesn't solve and often confounds the related difficulties. The problem is how to control those feelings of upset which are associated with those situations.

The starting point is to realize that you *learn* to get upset, and you can learn not to get upset or to be calm as well. Take the example of speaking in front of a group. If you are fearful in such a situation it is probably due to earlier experiences in similar situations wherein you were stressed in one way or another. You may have been criticized or made to feel stupid in front of your classmates; you may have been embarrassed in front of a group of relatives by some member of your family; you may have heard others talking about their fear of performing in group settings. Whatever the experience or series of experiences, you came to associate fearfulness with talking in front of a group. Going beyond that, you may have, because of your fear, been successful in avoiding such requirements in the past and, therefore, never learned how to get comfortable in such appearances. Uneasiness and tension are incompatible with calmness and relaxation; they cannot occur at the same time. One or the other sensation dominates, and your behavior reflects your condition.

Utilizing the principle of association discussed earlier, it becomes clear that the solution to such conditions of internal stress is found in associating relaxation with those situations which were previously associated with tension. Since tension and relaxation are incompatible, increasing one will decrease the other.

Because psychological tension corresponds to bodily tension, one way of establishing new associations is through increasing bodily relaxation in anxiety-provoking situations. The most effective procedure for accomplishing this is referred to as "systematic de-sensitization," meaning progressively pairing a state of relaxation with threatening situations until the relaxation displaces the anxiety in those situations.

Not long ago a young lady came to me for counseling because she was "deathly afraid" of insects, all kinds of insects. She would literally cross the street to avoid spiders, ants, or whatever. The problem was becoming unmanageable for her because her fears and the related behaviors were interfering with the ability to carry on her daily life in a reasonable fashion. She reported that her relatives and friends were becoming impatient with her and demanding that she stop the nonsense. Nonsense it was, and she knew it; but she could not control her fearfulness upon coming face to face with even the most harmless of creatures.

Discussion with this young woman about her early childhood revealed that she had had three or four bad experiences with insects, and that her mother was excessively concerned that her daughter keep clean and free of germs. The combined effect of early and ongoing experiences, including many avoidance behaviors, was growing more apparent as this young woman was becoming a responsible adult on whom others depended. Up until that time, much of the fearfulness was tolerated—and even unwittingly rewarded—because, as she put it, "girls are expected to be afraid of things like that."

A detailed history of the development of this problem is far too complex for presentation here, and it is really beside the point. The fact is that she had that anxiety in those situations, and the problem was one of teaching new associations by means of a systematic desensitization. The procedure was carried out by her in her natural environment, and the clinical situation was used for instructional purposes on how to go about it.

The first step was to teach her how to relax by tensing and relaxing various muscle groups in her body and associating pleasant thoughts (rustic scenes) and significant words ("warm," "calm," "relax") with the relaxed state. With sufficient practice, thinking those thoughts and saying those words brought about relaxation. We then discussed various activities that she could perform that were in some way related to insects. We considered drawing pictures of insects, reading stories about them, looking at pictures of them, and the like. In the earlier sessions we considered only slightly threatening activities and gradually moved toward direct contact with insects as therapy progressed.

The procedure involved getting this young lady to practice relaxing in the presence of progressively more threatening activities. As she learned to relax effectively in each insect-related situation, the remaining possible situations became less threatening. At the end of the progression, direct (reasonable) contact with insects was made possible with only minimal anxiety occurring.

This case history demonstrates the power and usefulness of internal stress-control techniques. If you learn to relax effectively, you can pair that relaxed state with situations that create stress, and you can diminish the stress as a result. These principles of association and incompatible-response practice can enable you to regulate those feelings that so often result in inappropriate and ineffective behaviors in relation to your children and other significant people in your life. Systematic desensitization is useful in any situation wherein you experience tension or anxiety, enabling you at least to regulate internal stress to reasonable levels. The procedure itself is as effective as you make it by specific and highly systematic application. If you decide to use it, probably the best approach is to contact a professional counselor who can provide guidance throughout the process. Like anything else, it will not work if it is not done correctly.

On a less involved level, it is beneficial to use these techniques routinely in your everyday experiences. If you find yourself becoming tense in any situation, it is often helpful to (1) take a deep breath, (2) think about something very pleasant for a few seconds, and (3) then deal with the situation which is creating the stress. Slowing yourself down and getting set in this simple manner often takes the edge off the stress and enables you to deal with the situation more calmly and, correspondingly, more effectively.

As suggested, the key to controlling stress reactions is relaxation. There are many popular techniques currently available which can be used to improve relaxation across life experiences. Deep muscle relaxation, transcendental meditation, self-hypnosis, and other approaches are all useful because they emphasize the development of relaxation skills as a natural part of an ongoing lifestyle. A more detailed discussion of such techniques can be found in those sources suggested at the end of this book.

Self-modification is basic to improvement in parent-child relationships. As suggested earlier, parents must change themselves if they expect to change their children. To the extent that you can improve your personal effectiveness, you will improve your effectiveness as a parent. Children who are fortunate enough to have effective parents will adjust more readily and themselves be well on their way toward effective parenthood.

Chapter 7

ISSUES AND ANSWERS

In the Preceding six chapters you have been provided with a significant amount of information about the behavioral approach to effective child rearing. This approach is not without its limitations and a considerable amount of controversy. The purpose of this final chapter is to provide a broad framework for effective use of behavior management and to clarify some of the basic issues related to its usefulness.

THE GOAL OF BEHAVIOR MANAGEMENT

Similar to all other approaches to child rearing, the purpose of the behavioral approach is to enable you, as a parent, to deal with your children most effectively to their and your benefit. It is not expected that you will sacrifice your life for their welfare nor, on the other hand, ignore their welfare for your own. Parenthood and childhood are give-and-take situations from which all should benefit and to which all must contribute. As a parent, the primary responsibility is yours. It is up to you to establish and maintain a workable partnership wherein greater responsibility carries with it more control. As the "junior partners" come to accept and fulfill increasing responsibilities, they then come to share more equally in the privileges of adulthood. Behavior management involves the provision of circumstances which enable the child to meet his parents'—and, increasingly, his own— reasonable expectations as he moves toward self-determination and responsibility.

The primary goal of your parenting efforts is, then, to maximize the potential of your children for becoming productive and contributing members of our society. That doesn't just happen. It depends on the effectiveness with which parents and significant educational and social institutions carry out the socialization process. At the earliest stages of infancy, and decreasingly as the individual grows and develops, the child depends on those around him to point the way toward productive individuality. He must learn the lessons of self-regulation and interdependence with others if he is to become socially and individually mature and actualized.

Much has been written and said about this process of socialization through child management. Opinions vary widely on what is "best for the child." Too often, however, there is minimum regard for what is best for the parent also—as if the welfare of one necessarily contradicts the welfare of the other. The behavioral approach adapts well to the conception of parenthood and childhood together—"peoplehood." The techniques of the approach are such that they emphasize the consideration of the needs of all concerned in any given situation. The focus is on behavior and its regulation and modification through a workable understanding of the nature of human (adult and child) behavior.

MISCONCEPTIONS

Contrary to what some of the critics of the behavioral approach have suggested, the behavior management system is not irrevocably dictatorial and malevolent in design. Like any other approach to anything, however, there is potential for abuse of the principles of influence contained within the system. The focus is on control or regulation of behavior, but the intent of such manipulation implied within that framework is for the welfare of all concerned. In spite of that pervasive intention, the notion of control is often viewed as aversive and threatening from a democratic perspective. What we often fail to realize, however, is that controls, in one form or another, are all around us. The real issue does not seem to be whether we influence others and ourselves, but, rather, whether we do it systematically. When the notions of premeditation and design come into play in our interactions with others, children and adults, the presumptions of exploitation are typically not far behind. This is unfortunate. But it is overemphasized by those who would deny the fact of pervasive controls in our everyday existence.

Personal Freedom

Effective child rearing does not contradict the existence of and necessity for individual freedom. It does, however, prepare the growing child for expression of that freedom from a realistic and socially responsible perspective. Just as the parents do not use their position of greater influence to exploit the child, the child comes to regulate his behaviors with an eye toward the needs and rights of others. Personal freedom really means the ability to meet one's own needs responsibly and, subsequently, to share in the satisfaction of the needs of others for the welfare of all concerned.

The opportunity for personal freedom, or self-regulation, begins with external control, and the first and most significant products of that control come through interaction with parents. The behavioral management system provides you with not only a blueprint for establishing effective controls but also the means by which to foster personal freedom in your children.

The Roots of Behavior

Traditionally, human behaviors have been considered external representations of mysterious and unknowable processes within the individual. Countless years have been spent in investigations of those underlying forces, and all sorts of ideas and theories have been proposed to account for them, with varying success. Until recently, however, the major facts (human behavior) of such investigations have often been considered only indirectly related to the "more important" issues. This interesting and perplexing tendency to discount what we see and feel is not continued in the behavioral approach. What a person does is, to a great extent, what that person is. The roots of behavior are found in what the person gets for what he does, and the key to raising effective individuals is found in giving what is needed upon getting what is required.

The Natural Parent

One of the most common misconceptions about the behavioral approach to child rearing is that it is not natural. It is sometimes suggested that the parent will become a robot, reacting to his children without spontaneity and always being preoccupied with the technology of manipulation. This is far-fetched and naïve. The fact is that the various principles of behavior modification are used all of the time to varying degrees and with varying effectiveness. The only significant change proposed by the approach is that the principles be used systematically so that the effects can be regulated toward desirable outcomes. In the early stages of change you may feel awkward and uncertain about your actions, and spontaneity at that point may be impaired. That occurs with the development of any new skill until it becomes stabilized. Beyond that point the return to normal becomes apparent, and you are then in a position to be naturally consistent and increasingly effective.

To most of us, it is not surprising that many roles that we play in our everyday adult lives require some type of formal training and certification. Much employment is regulated by the strict requirement that the employee be prepared for his function. And yet when we look at the role of parent, there is no prerequisite, no assurance that the critical job to be performed will benefit the society for which that child is being prepared. Objection to systematically effective child management procedures is, from this perspective, self-defeating.

Bribery, Coercion, and Punishment

The behavioral approach to child management is, above all, a positive approach that emphasizes positive outcomes for desirable behaviors. The focus is on reward and its usefulness in building effective and adaptive behavior patterns in children and adults. As you know from your own experience with children, however, it is impossible to avoid completely the use of punishment in some management situations. Punishment is the most effective means of stopping a behavior abruptly, and there are some situations where there is really no other recourse.

The most obvious of such situations involves the child's endangerment of himself or someone else through his actions. The young child running into the street without looking is a good example. Punishment is typically called for in that situation so as to avoid disaster. Of course even in that situation the behavioral parent combines the punishment outcome with a positive outcome for not running into the street. In any event, punishment is used only sparingly and as a last resort. With this consideration in mind, the important point becomes one of how to punish most effectively when necessary, and guidelines for that are provided in Chapter 1.

At the other extreme, questions are often raised regarding the use of reinforcement to get children to behave in desirable ways. The most common objection raised has to do with the notion of bribery. As pointed out in Chapter 1, reward is not bribery, for the objective of reward is to enable the child to learn the most desirable behaviors for the welfare of all concerned. It would be nice if people behaved appropriately just because they were supposed to, but it doesn't work that way. Behavior is outcome-directed, and the only way to regulate it is through regulation of those outcomes. Such regulation is the nature of behavior management.

Finally, the behavioral approach is not coercive. The uses of the various outcomes described in the preceding chapters are educational and supportive, enabling the child to develop his potential within the limits of a social context. The emphasis should not be on forcing the child to comply with rigid and arbitrary parental dictates but, rather, on enabling the child to develop those behaviors by which he can best meet his needs with appropriate consideration of the rights and needs of others. The behavioral approach points the way most clearly and consistently for the child, whose limited experience does not yet allow for more independent self-regulation.

LIMITATIONS

The behavioral management approach is not and is not meant to be portrayed as the last word in child rearing. It is effective without question, but its degree of effectiveness is determined by the strengths of those who implement the system and by the overriding complexity of human behavior. Current research in behavior management reveals that the most consistent and significant results of behavior control are found in settings where the managers have the greatest control over the environment in which the individuals reside. These findings are consistent with the basic principle of behavior management: you control an individual's behavior to the extent that you control his environment. In the natural environment, it is apparent that total control over anyone's environment is impossible and undesirable (because of the unfortunate potential for abuse). As a parent, however, you can see that you do regulate much of what your child needs and desires, and it is through the intelligent and humanistic regulation of those outcomes that you exert influence. The durability of that influence depends on its early effectiveness in enabling your children to meet their needs in a reasonable fashion. As the child comes out from under that direct influence and becomes subject to other sources of influence, including his internal regulation, he will reflect in his behavior what he has learned from you.

A POINT OF VIEW

Over the past several years of psychological consultation many parents have asked me to express an opinion on the general nature of parenthood. After some consideration of that topic, I have formulated a position that reflects what I consider to be a reasonable point of view.

Parents are responsible for the existence and welfare of their children. They represent to those children the nature of the world within which they must adapt and grow. In that capacity, the parent is the authority to which the child is initially responsible and from whom he gains his knowledge of and capability for an effective lifestyle. Parents are, by the nature of their roles, authoritarians. They are in charge, and they are models of benevolent control. In that position, they are a team that must work together in presenting to the children a consistent framework for regulation of behavior in compliance with what they judge to be appropriate and good. They are not, in that sense, equals, and they should not strive to engender such equality.

The behavior management system presented in this book requires an understanding of the nature of human behavior and capability for utilizing that understanding in fostering in children appropriate behaviors that will enable them to realize their potential as human beings. You have the authority to implement that approach and the responsibility to do it well.

Best of luck!

GLOSSARY

ASSOCIATION   The connections made between behaviors and situations due to the simultaneous occurrence or existence of those behaviors and situations. Increases the likelihood of future simultaneous occurrences.

ATTITUDE   A feeling, disposition, or orientation toward persons or situations.

AVOIDANCE BEHAVIOR   Acting in such a manner as to postpone or avert the presentation of an aversive situation.

BACK-UP REINFORCER   That desirable outcome which can be obtained by cashing in tokens or points earned in the token economy or similar program.

BEHAVIOR ANTICIPATION   Restructuring of situations so as to prevent the occurrence of typical undesirable behaviors in those situations.

BEHAVIOR REHEARSAL   Imagined or actual practice of a behavior in preparation for the performance of that behavior in the natural environment. Also called dramatization.

BEHAVIORAL CONTRACT   A formal agreement made by two or more persons in which the desired and/or undesired behaviors and their consequences are specified. Also called contingency contract.

BEHAVIORAL GOAL   The objective, described in terms of actual behaviors involved, toward which the management plan is directed.

BRIBERY   Payment in some form to someone for performance of acts potentially harmful to himself and/or others and in violation of some social standard.

CONDITIONED RESPONSE   A reflex behavior brought about by a situation that has gained the power to elicit the response through association with an unconditioned stimulus (as an eyeblink conditioned to a sound that has been associated with a bright light).

CONDITIONED STIMULUS   A previously neutral stimulus that has gained, by association with an unconditioned stimulus, the power to bring about a reflex response.

CONDITIONING   The behavior-change process involving the arrangement of concurrent and/or consequent conditions.

CONTINGENCY   The relationship between a given behavior and its outcome.

CONTINGENCY CONTRACT   See BEHAVIORAL CONTRACT.

CONTINUOUS REINFORCEMENT   A schedule whereby each response is reinforced. Used in early stages of response acquisition. See POSITIVE REINFORCEMENT AND NEGATIVE REINFORCEMENT.

CUE   A stimulus that signals that reinforcement will follow a particular response (as a red light is a cue for stopping).

DESENSITIZATION   The systematic occurrence of a relaxation response in the presence of circumstances that previously brought about tension or anxiety. Begun in slightly anxiety-provoking and gradually increased to highly anxiety-provoking situations. Relaxation displaces tension. Also called systematic desensitization.

DIFFERENTIAL REINFORCEMENT   The reinforcement of a particular response in some situations and not in others, leading to consistent performance of that response in those situations.

DRAMATIZATION   See BEHAVIOR REHEARSAL.

ELICIT   To bring about a response automatically.

EMIT   To respond voluntarily; response is influenced by its outcome.

EXTINCTION   *See* ZERO OUTCOME.

FADING   Gradual removal of cues or prompts that signal or help initiate a response.

HIGH PROBABILITY BEHAVIOR   A response that occurs with high frequency when the individual is allowed to select from among several alternatives. *See* PREMACK PRINCIPLE.

INCOMPATIBLE BEHAVIOR   Behavior that is inconsistent with an undesired response and that is reinforced to reduce its incompatible alternative.

INTERMITTENT REINFORCEMENT   A reinforcement schedule in which a response is rewarded only on some occurrences. Used in later stages of behavior change to increase durability of responses. *See* REINFORCEMENT.

INTERNAL EVENTS   Responses occurring within the individual and which may be altered through self-management techniques.

INTERNAL STRESS CONTROL   The self-management of internal stress reactions by displacement with incompatible internal states.

MODELING   Acquisition of a new behavior through observation of that behavior and its outcome in someone else. Also called observational learning.

NEGATIVE REINFORCEMENT   The removal of something aversive following a behavior for the purpose of strengthening that behavior. *See* REWARD OUTCOME.

OBSERVATIONAL LEARNING   *See* MODELING.

OPERANT BEHAVIOR   Emitted behavior that is controlled by its outcomes.

PERSONALITY   That pattern of behaviors characteristic of an individual.

POSITIVE AVOIDANCE   Removal of oneself from a situation so as to avoid inadvertant reinforcement of undesirable behaviors in others.

POSITIVE REINFORCEMENT   Addition of something desirable following a behavior for the purpose of strengthening that behavior. *See* REWARD OUTCOME.

PREMACK PRINCIPLE   The principle that states that if performance of a high probability behavior is made contingent on performance of a lower probability behavior, the higher will reinforce the lower, resulting in an increase in the frequency of the lower.

PROMPT   An event that helps initiate a response (instructions, gestures, etc.).

PUNISHMENT OUTCOME   Addition of something aversive or removal of something positive following a behavior for the purpose of weakening that behavior.

REINFORCEMENT

RESPONDENT BEHAVIOR   Elicited behavior that is controlled by antecedent stimuli.

RESPONSE COST   A punishment procedure in which something positive is lost or removed as an outcome of the performance of an undesirable behavior.

REWARD OUTCOME   An event following a behavior that serves to increase or strengthen that behavior.

SATIATION   The excessive use of desirable outcome until that outcome becomes less desirable or no longer reinforcing.

SELF-OBSERVATION   The self-management technique of recording one's own behavior.

SELF-TALK   Instructions given to oneself in order to prepare oneself for behavior and/or to reward oneself for appropriate behaviors.

SHAPING   Building a new behavior by rewarding successive approximations toward that behavior.

SITUATION CONTROL   The self-management technique of allowing certain behaviors to occur only in certain situations.

SYSTEMATIC DESENSITIZATION   *See* DESENSITIZATION.

TARGET BEHAVIOR   That specific behavior which is to be changed by means of behavior management strategies.

THOUGHT CONTROL   The self-management technique of regulating thoughts about certain behaviors. *See* SELF-TALK.

THOUGHT STOPPING   *See* THOUGHT CONTROL.

TIME-OUT   A punishment outcome wherein the individual is temporarily removed from the reinforcing environment following some undesirable act.

UNCONDITIONED RESPONSE   A response naturally elicited by an unconditioned stimulus (as perspiration is elicited by heat).

UNCONDITIONED STIMULUS   A stimulus that naturally elicits an unconditioned reflex response.

VICARIOUS REINFORCEMENT   The indirect reinforcing effect on one person due to his observation of the direct reinforcement effect on another. *See* MODELING.

ZERO OUTCOME   Doing nothing following a behavior that has previously been reinforced for the purpose of weakening that behavior. Also called extinction.

SUGGESTED READING

For parents interested in becoming thoroughly familiar with the behavioral management system, there are several books available which provide additional information along with excellent examples of application. From among those available, the author has selected ten of the best. They are listed below.

1. *Home Token Economy: An Incentive Program for Children and Their Parents,* Alvord; Research Press, Champaign, Illinois, 1973.

2. *Parents Are Teachers: A Child Management Program,* Becker; Research Press, 1971.

3. *New Tools for Changing Behavior,* Deibert and Harmon; Research Press, 1973.

4. *Changing Children's Behavior,* Krumboltz and Krumboltz; Prentice-Hall, Inc., Englewood Cliffs, New Jersey, 1972.

5. *Elementary Principles of Behavior,* Whaley and Malott; Behaviordelia, Kalamazoo, Michigan, 1970.

6. *For Love of Children: Behavioral Psychology for Parents*, McIntire; CRM Books, Del Mar, California, 1970.

7. *Families: Applications of Social Learning to Family Life*, Patterson; Research Press, 1971.

8. *Living with Children*, Patterson and Gullion; Research Press, 1971.

9. *Modifying Children's Behavior: A Guide for Parents and Professionals*, Valett; Fearon Publishers, Palo Alto, California, 1969.

10. *You Can Help Your Child Improve Study and Homework Behaviors*, Zifferblatt; Research Press, 1970.

For parents interested in self-management techniques, a growing number of related books is available. From among those currently in print, the author has selected ten of the best. They are listed below.

1. Cotler and Guerra. *Assertion Training: A Humanistic-Behavioral Guide to Self-Dignity.* Champaign, Ill: Research Press, 1976.

2. Karlins and Andrews. *Biofeedback: Turning on the Power of Your Mind.* New York: Warner, 1973.

3. Mahoney and Mahoney. *Permanent Weight Control.* New York: Norton, 1976.

4. Mahoney and Thoresen, editors. *Self-Control: Power to the Person.* Monterey: Brooks/Cole, 1974.

5. McMullin and Casey. *Talk Sense to Yourself.* Champaign, Ill.: Research Press, 1976.

6. Read. *Childbirth without Fear: The Principles and Practice of Natural Childbirth.* New York: Harper & Row, 1959.

7. Stuart and Davis. *Slim Chance in a Fat World: Behavioral Control of Obesity.* Champaign, Ill.: Research Press, 1972.

8. Thoresen and Mahoney. *Behavioral Self-Control.* New York: Holt, Rinehart and Winston, 1974.

9. Watson and Tharp. *Self-Directed Behavior: Self-Modification for Personal Adjustment.* Monterey: Brooks/Cole, 1972.

10. Williams and Long. *Toward a Self-Managed Life Style.* Boston: Houghton Mifflin, 1975.

GENERAL READING

Listed below are several books selected with helping professionals, as well as parents, in mind. Included are works presenting both theoretical and practical approaches for use with parents, teachers, students, and individuals seeking professional counseling services. These references provide a wealth of information about all aspects of the behavioral approach to human behavior.

1. Abidin. *Parenting Skills: Trainer's Manual and Workbook.* New York: Behavioral Publications, 1976.

2. Ackerman. *Operant Conditioning Techniques for the Classroom Teacher.* Glenview, Ill.: Scott, Foresman, 1972.

3. Ashem and Poser. *Adaptive Learning: Behavior Modification with Children.* New York: Pergamon Press, 1973.

4. Ayllon and Azrin. *The Token Economy: A Motivational System for Therapy and Rehabilitation.* New York: Appleton-Century-Crofts, 1968.

5. Bandura. *Principles of Behavior Modification.* New York: Holt, Rinehart and Winston, 1969.

6. Becker and Becker. *Successful Parenthood.* Champaign, Ill.: Research Press, 1976.

7. Becker, Thomas, and Carnine. *Reducing Behavior Problems: An Operant Conditioning Guide for Teachers.* Urbana: Educational Resources, 1969.

8. Berne. *What Do You Do After You Say Hello?* New York: Grove Press, 1972.

9. Bing. *Six Practical Lessons to an Easy Childbirth.* New York: Grosset & Dunlap, 1967.

10. Blackham and Silberman. *Modification of Child and Adolescent Behavior.* Belmont, Cal.: Wadsworth, 1975.

11. Bootzin. *Behavior Modification and Therapy: An Introduction.* Cambridge, Mass: Winthrop, 1975.

12. Bradfield, Editor. *Behavior Modification: The Human Effort,* San Rafael, Calif.: Dimensions, 1970.

13. Browning and Stover. *Behavior Modification in Child Treatment.* Chicago: Aldine-Atherton, 1971.

14. Buckley and Walker. *Modifying Classroom Behavior: A Manual of Procedure for Classroom Teachers.* Champaign, Ill.: Research Press, 1970.

15. Clarizio. *Toward Positive Classroom Discipline.* New York: John Wiley, 1971.

16. Dollar. *Humanizing Classroom Discipline: A Behavioral Approach.* New York: Harper & Row, 1972.

17. Dunn, editor. *Smoking Behavior: Motives and Incentives.* New York: John Wiley, 1973.

18. Fargo, Behrns, and Nolen, editors. *Behavior Modification in the Classroom.* Belmont, Cal.: Wadsworth, 1970.

19. Franks, editor. *Behavior Therapy: Appraisal and Status.* New York: McGraw-Hill, 1969.

20. Gardner. *Behavior Modification: Applications in Mental Retardation.* Chicago: Aldine-Atherton, 1971.

21. Gelfand. *Social Learning in Childhood.* Monterey: Brooks/Cole, 1969.

22. Glaser, editor. *The Nature of Reinforcement.* New York: Academic Press, 1971.

23. Gnagey. *How to Put Up with Parents: A Guide for Teenagers.* Champaign, Ill.: Research Press, 1976.

24. Goldstein, Heller, and Sechrist. *Psychotherapy and the Psychology of Behavior Change.* New York: John Wiley, 1966.

25. Graubard and Rosenberg. *Classrooms that Work.* New York: E. P. Dutton, 1974.

26. Guerney. *Psychotherapeutic Agents: New Roles for Nonprofes-*

sionals, Parents, and Teachers. New York: Holt, Rinehart and Winston, 1969.

27. Haring and Phillips. *An Analysis and Modification of Classroom Behavior.* Englewood Cliffs, N.J.: Prentice-Hall, 1972.

28. Homme. *How to Use Contingency Contracting in the Classroom.* Champaign, Ill.: Research Press, 1969.

29. Homme and Tosti. *Behavior Technology: Motivation and Contingency Management.* San Rafael, Cal.: Individual Learning Systems, 1971.

30. Hunter. *Reinforcement Theory for Teachers.* El Segundo, Calif.: Tip Publications, 1967.

31. Jacobs and Spradlin, editors. *The Group as Agent of Change.* New York: Behavioral Publications, 1974.

32. Kanfer and Goldstein, editors. *Helping People Change.* New York: Pergamon Press, 1975.

33. Kincaid. *A Walden Two Experiment.* New York: William Morrow, 1973.

34. Kounin. *Discipline and Group Management in Classrooms.* New York: Holt, Rinehart and Winston, 1970.

35. Krumboltz and Thoresen, editors. *Behavioral Counseling: Case Studies and Techniques.* New York: Holt, Rinehart and Winston, 1969.

36. London. *Behavior Control.* New York: Harper & Row, 1969.

37. Lovibond. *Conditioning and Enuresis.* New York: Pergamon Press, 1964.

38. Madsen and Madsen. *Parents—Children—Discipline: A Positive Approach.* Boston: Allyn and Bacon, 1970.

39. Madsen and Madsen. *Teaching/Discipline: Behavioral Principles Toward a Positive Approach.* Boston: Allyn and Bacon, 1970.

40. Mahoney. *Cognition and Behavior Modification.* Cambridge, Mass.: Ballinger, 1974.

41. McConnell. *Understanding Human Behavior.* New York: Holt, Rinehart and Winston, 1974.

42. Mikulas. *Behavior Modification: An Overview.* New York: Harper & Row, 1972.

43. Miller. *Systematic Parent Training: Procedures, Cases and Issues.* Champaign, Ill.: Research Press, 1976.

44. Miller. *Principles of Everyday Behavior Analysis.* Monterey: Brooks/Cole, 1974.

45. Neisworth and Smith. *Modifying Retarded Behavior.* Boston: Houghton Mifflin, 1973.

46. O'Leary and O'Leary, editors. *Classroom Management.* New York: Pergamon, 1972.

47. Patterson. *Families: Applications of Social Learning to Family Life. Champaign, Ill.: Research Press, 1971.*

48. Paul and Bernstein. *Anxiety and Behavior: Treatment by Systematic Desensitization and Related Techniques.* New York: General Learning Press, 1973.

49. Payne, Polloway, Kaufman, and Scranton. *Living in the Classroom: The Currency-Based Token Economy.* New York: Behavioral Publications, 1976.

50. Pizzat. *Behavior Modification in Residential Treatment for Children: Model of a Program.* New York: Behavioral Publications, 1973.

51. Ramp and Semb, editors. *Behavioral Analysis and Education.* Englewood Cliffs, N.J.: Prentice-Hall, 1975.

52. Reynolds. *A Primer of Operant Conditioning.* Chicago: Scott, Foresman, 1968.

53. Rickard, editor. *Behavioral Intervention in Human Problems.* New York: Pergamon Press, 1971.

54. Robinson. *Effective Study.* New York: Harper & Row, 1970.

55. Sarason, Glaser, and Fargo. *Reinforcing Productive Classroom Behavior: Teacher's Guide to Behavior Modification.* New York: Behavioral Publications, 1971.

56. Sherman. *Behavior Modification: Theory and Practice.* Belmont, Cal.: Wadsworth Publishing Company, 1973.

57. Shostrom. *Man, the Manipulator.* New York: Bantam Books, 1968.

58. Skinner. *About Behaviorism.* New York: Alfred A. Knopf, 1974.

59. Skinner. *Beyond Freedom and Dignity.* New York: Alfred A. Knopf, 1971.

60. Skinner. *Walden II.* New York: Macmillan, 1948.

61. Smith and Smith. *Child Management: A Program for Parents and Teachers.* Ann Arbor: Ann Arbor Publishers, 1966.

62. Sobey. *The Nonprofessional Revolution in Mental Health.* New York: Columbia University Press, 1970.

63. Stuart. *Trick or Treatment: How and When Psychotherapy Fails.* Champaign, Ill.: Research Press, 1970.

64. Sundel and Sundel. *Behavior Modification in the Human Services: A Systematic Introduction to Concepts and Applications.* New York: John Wiley, 1975.

65. Tharp and Wetzel. *Behavior Modification in the Natural Environment.* New York: Academic Press, 1969.

66. Travers. *Essentials of Learning.* New York: Macmillan, 1972.

67. Ullmann and Krasner. *Case Studies in Behavior Modification.* New York: Holt, Rinehart and Winston, 1965.

68. Valett. *Prescriptions for Learning: A Parent's Guide to Remedial Home Training.* Belmont, Cal.: Fearon Publishers, 1970.

69. Vernon. *Motivating Children: Behavior Modification in the Classroom.* New York: Holt, Rinehart and Winston, 1972.

70. Watson. *Child Behavior Modification.* New York: Pergamon Press, 1973.

71. Wenrich. *A Primer of Behavior Modification.* Monterey: Brooks/Cole, 1970.

72. Whaley and Malott. *Elementary Principles of Behavior.* New York: Appleton-Century-Crofts, 1971.

73. Wheeler, editor. *Beyond the Punitive Society.* San Francisco: W. H. Freeman, 1973.

74. Williams. *Operant Learning: Procedures for Changing Behavior.* Monterey: Brooks/Cole, 1973.

75. Yates. *Behavior Therapy.* New York: John Wiley, 1970.

INDEX